The War Within

MY STORY

JOSIF WRIGHT

ISBN 978-1-64416-028-2 (paperback)
ISBN 978-1-64416-029-9 (digital)

Christian Faith Publishing, Inc.
832 Park Avenue
Meadville, PA 16335
www.christianfaithpublishing.com

All quotes at the beginning of each chapter are from Josif Wright, unless noted.

Some of the names in this book have been changed.

All scripture references are from New King James Version (NKJV) or English Standard Version (ESV).

Printed in the United States of America

Ryan is an inspiration to all who know him. His journey has led him down some dark paths where he has met and battled evil face to face, of which many have not come back alive. The enemy has been strong and persistent, but with his young faith and commitment to the Lord, Ryan has held his own. The battle has been hard and has taken its toll, but Ryan has persevered and has overcome great odds. His desire is strong and his heart is determined to finish this battle that is set before him! Even though the enemy sought to destroy this young man, he knows God has a different plan. His story will encourage and empower all who struggle, and also those who have loved ones who struggle in similar battles. This young man has a story to tell!

—Scott Myers, Ph.D., L.C.C.C.
Founder, Life House Ministries, Inc.

This book answers the question, "is God really there?" Often during conflict or trouble, we ask that very question. It is only after the conflict has passed, that we can see that God was moving all the time. This book is a testament of this very fact. The War Within: My Story is just another proof that God can and will get you through anything and strengthen you as He does. God bless you as you read this book, that you may see yourself in the process.

—Rev. Gary L. Pickard
Liberty Baptist Church

I remember the first time I saw Ryan. He was attending one of my classes at The Turning Point Foundation. As I glanced around the room, I noticed a new face; not just any face, but a face with a smile that lit up the room. As I got to know Ryan I observed that his grandiose smile was the personification of his whole personality. He was a delightful young man who was warm and caring with an infectious personality that drew people to him.

Early on, you could feel a tremendous anointing on his life. With a great anointing often comes a great attack. Ryan was certainly under attack from Satan. He was in a life or death struggle for his life. Bad choices and inner demons that did not want to let him go. As time went on and my relationship with Ryan grew, I noticed that he started to turn the tide of addiction in his life. He started to realize, and walk in authority given him under the Blood of Jesus. It is a beautiful thing to watch someone transform right in front of your eyes.

Now I see that anointing operating openly in Ryan's life. I have been blessed to see what God has done in Ryan, and I am excited to see what God has in store next. I am proud to call him my friend.

—David Pendley
Executive Director, Turning Point Foundation

Having walked through the intake process with hundreds of worried parents who were sending their child into rehab, I understand the fear, worry and shame that comes with it. For those of you in this situation, this book is for you. At the very least, it brings comfort to know that you are not alone in this walk; at the very height, it brings confidence that God can and will heal your loved one. To the churchgoing believer who is hiding the truth of a child's addiction, please pick up this book. You are not the first Christian parent faced with this battle. Ryan and his family have been there and they have come through on the other side. In his book, The War Within: My Story, Josif shares his anguish, doubts, fears and ultimate joy with the reader to bring hope and focus on Jesus as the battle is waged. Victory can be yours as well!

—Mary Louise Fiddler
House of Hope, Facility Administrator

From the moment I started reading the first paragraph of The War Within: My Story, I was gripped & inspired. I couldn't stop reading, and was looking for more to read! I loved it!

This book, The War Within: My Story, will save lives. It will save families and give the brokenhearted hope.

—Corporal Benny P. Washington, Sr.
UAB Police, Hospital Operations

To the memory of Eric Lawrence Thomas.
Rest in the arms of Jesus, my friend.

Finally, be strong in the Lord and in the strength of his might. Put on the whole armor of God, that you may be able to stand against the schemes of the devil. For we wrestle not against flesh and blood, but against the rulers, against the authorities, against the cosmic powers over this present darkness, against the spiritual forces of evil in the heavenly places. Therefore take up the whole armor of God, that you may be able to withstand in the evil day, and having done all, to stand firm.

—Ephesians 6:10–13 (ESV)

Contents

Acknowledgments

I can't possibly name everyone who prayed for us during our many times of need. There are just too many to count. I do want to thank the thousands of people who asked God to open the floodgates of heaven and outpour His love, mercy, and grace upon Ryan and our family. There are a few, however, that were absolutely pivotal in our processes of grieving, seeking help, and healing. You didn't judge us; you just prayed for God's intervention. Thank you for standing (and kneeling) with us in prayer, Charles Alford II, Johnny Arnett, Justin Barrett, Ray Bozeman, Mark Cahill, Victor Castro, Claudio Cruz, Connie and Jody Dyess, Frances Fawehinmi, Stephen Herd (St. Christopher's), Rock Hobbs, Keith Jackson, Karen Katchuk, Ken and Becky Knight, Jason Love, Ron Luster, Scott Manns, Tommy Maxwell, Jesus Rodriguez, David Surber, Kris Washington, Jarret Williamson, and Janet Woodham.

Hundreds of churches were represented by those who prayed for us as well. Thank you to all of the specific churches that prayed for us, lifting our needs to the heavenly Father. Several churches have, in one way or another, reached out physically to my family and provided much needed encouragement and love. You are the hands and feet of Jesus: 3Circle Church (Thomasville, Alabama), Bethel Baptist (Thorsby, Alabama), Casa de Luz (Elberta, Alabama), Calvary Chapel (Adelanto, California), Canaan Baptist Church (Bessemer, Alabama), Church of the Highlands (Birmingham, Alabama), and Oasis of Praise (Bessemer, Alabama).

There were those who were there in the thick of it all with us. Those who visited, called, prayed, counseled with, and physically took part toward our journey of redemption. I simply cannot thank you enough for being there for us and experiencing our heartaches and our joys with us: John Beck, Jean Berefield, Joey Captain, Lindsey Brooke Davis, Oscar and Carolyn Davis, Keith and Yonna Davis, Valerie Davis, Beth Defranco, John Dowling, Josh Easterling, Rick and Mary Louise Fiddler, Jimmy and Tracey Gullatte, Judy Gunstream, Brett Green, Heath and Brianna Hancock, Tal Hayes, Tim Hendrix Jr., Tim Hendrix Sr., Jonathan Hicks, Rock Hobbs, Dennis Hollins, Chris and Diane Horton, Rick Kornis, Mark Lambert, Rebekah Laws, John Lewis, Rachel Meadors, Jared Murray, Ray Norris, Scott Myers, Chris Parr, Ty Parten, Dave Pendley, Ray Perea, Gary and Kathy Pickard, Jeremy Reyer, Keith Russell, Raul Aguilar Salazar, Dr. Al Saunders, Dr. Ted and Betty Shelton, David Steen, Dr. Eric Thomas, This'l (Travis Tyler), Jon Wallace, Allison Walls, Lamar Ward, Justin Warren, Benny Paul Washington, Don Wheat, Dr. Jack Whites, Carol Wright, Jack and Cheryl Wright, Stepheni Wright, Rachel Wright, and Wayne Wright.

Thank you to those who we met and worked at rehabilitation facilities, desiring to do all that they can to help those caught in addiction. Your tireless hours, weeks, months, and years will be rewarded for all of those you have sought to reach. God bless you all at The Journey (Troy, Alabama), House of Hope (Adelanto, California), Bradford (Warrior, Alabama), and Turning Point Foundation (Thorsby, Alabama)

Thank you to Christian Faith Publishing for accepting, and being willing to publish my story. This journey all started with you, Justine Muller. Thank you!

Most of all, thank you, Jesus, for all You have brought my family through and taught us during those very treacherous years. Thank you for Your grace, love, and mercy that upheld us through it all. Thank you for the strength to keep fighting in this war when I had nothing left, and thank you for the countless miracles, signs, and rescues that You made possible. Help us to each fulfill our purpose on this planet, reaching out to others in need and making an eternal difference. Then we will happily enter heaven after we draw our last breath here. Thank you, Jesus, my Healer, my Deliverer, my Provider, and my Savior!

Introduction

I'm a private person. I don't particularly like sharing painful stories about my life. As a matter of fact, I don't want other people knowing my business. My family and I can deal with certain situations that come up in our lives, even asking close friends to pray and believing that God will help us. Handling our issues without others knowing the details is how I would prefer it to be. But there has been a prodding by the Holy Spirit to share my story. Why would I do such a thing and open myself up to criticism, ridicule, and judgment from other people? Well, as I was thinking about these questions, the Lord spoke to me, saying, "Actually, this life is not about you, Josif. It's not about what others say about you, and it's not about you being comfortable. It's about you being obedient to Me and using the difficult circumstances you've gone through in life to reach out to others with the soul saving Gospel of Jesus Christ. How am I going to respond to that? I'm going to be obedient, follow where the Lord leads, and say what the Lord wants me to say.

The souls of people are at stake every day. Thousands of people all across planet Earth die each day. I feel a sense of urgency to share with people the hope that only Jesus can give because time is definitely running out. If someone reads this book and stays away from drugs, the effort will be worth it. If someone reads this book, and it helps them to better deal with a loved one that is addicted to drugs, the effort will be worth it. If someone reads this book and gives their life to Jesus, the effort will definitely be worth it. I have seen things that no dad should see. I have experienced things that have shaken me to my core. There are images that, to this day, I'm trying to erase from my mind. There are some things that I have experienced and seen that aren't in this book and will never be talked about by me to anyone. However, if it were not for these terrible things that have happened to me and my family, I don't know if I would love Jesus and other people like I do now.

It is a fact that every human being is fighting their own battles, sometimes on a daily basis. Some fight physical battles such as a disease, an infirmity, or another health issue. Others fight those invisible battles that people around them know nothing about. Fear, depression, anxiety, pride, envy, and hatred are silent killers to the soul that can easily lead to mental, emotional, spiritual, and even physical problems. Still, others fight battles of addiction such as drugs, food, tobacco, alcohol, gambling, and cigarettes. These addictions often lead to physical problems very quickly and can kill you sooner or later. Addictions can alter who you are and how you act, sometimes to the point that you lose your very identity. If not faced head-on and dealt with, all of these battles can render you helpless and unable to function in life. There is a war that is being waged. If we could physically see the spiritual warfare that goes on all around us, it might scare us to death! The war is real, and battles are fought on a daily basis not only for the souls of people, but also for people's testimonies and futures on this earth. When our lives are turned into war zones, we must fight and not give up.

After going through all that I've been through in the last eight to nine years, I certainly have a much better understanding of what it means to "fight the good fight of faith." As in the biblical story of the Prodigal Son, the son made the impulsive, selfish, and foolish choice of leaving home to spend his inheritance on riotous living. My very own flesh and blood did the same. Pain medication, OxyContin, cocaine, heroin, rebellion, and disobedience plagued our lives for many years. Some things we knew about; some things we found out later. Other things, I don't even want to know about. It has been a ride that I wouldn't wish on my worst enemy. However, in the midst of it all, God gave me the grace to endure and the courage to fight. Through all of my sleepless nights, crying out to God for help on my knees and my face to the floor praying for deliverance, God gave me the peace to know that He would redeem and restore. In those times when I wanted to give up on life, God always gave me the strength to keep pressing forward to fight and win the war within. He will give you that very same strength and courage in any situation you may face.

1

The Call

*Life can change in a moment. When tough times come, ask
God for wisdom then stand your ground and fight.*

The year 2010 proved to be a very trying year. Neither church work
nor my job teaching at school was going very well. Our home became
a place where battles were being fought daily. My entire life was a
war zone. My son, Ryan, began hanging around older guys who had
sketchy reputations. Ryan was a senior in high school, and these guys
were several years older. He seemed to be drifting away from God
and from our family. The baseball scholarship that he really wanted
just wasn't that important anymore. Those things were red flags to
me and my wife, Bethany. We did the best we could to steer him
away from these guys and back to God. Aside from these older guys
he was hanging around with, there really weren't many other red flags
though. Some things seemed a little out of the ordinary, but we were
dealing with a teenager so the unordinary was sometimes ordinary,
if you know what I mean. Ryan's grades were as good as ever, and
things were fairly normal. Bethany and I did start to dread weekends
because there were so many arguments about where he was going and
who he'd be hanging out with.

"Where did all of this come from?" I'd ask myself. Over a short
amount of time, things started falling apart at home. Bethany and I

couldn't believe it. Here we were, trying our best to raise our children in the *admonition of the Lord*, and things were getting worse. I always thought that if we loved the Lord and taught our children to follow Jesus, things would be fine. We would have a problem here and there but nothing major. Wow, was I clueless!

My mother, Shirley, died from *Clostridium difficile* brought on by multiple myeloma on January 2, 2008. This was a huge blow to my children, Ryan and Rebekah. They loved their grandmama so much and had so many happy memories of spending time with her. Looking back, I don't think that they really took time to grieve properly and celebrate her life. We went back to school soon after the funeral and got back into regular routines. We should've talked and expressed our feelings to each other more. We should've talked more about all of the happy times that we had with her and how blessed we were to have had her in our lives for so many years. It seemed as though Ryan couldn't handle the anger that he was feeling and the loss that he was experiencing.

Things at home were not great, but they were fairly stable, I thought. Then came the call—the call that would bring me to my knees and start a chain reaction of hellish years on earth. It was November 22, 2010. I was teaching school when word came from the office that I had an important call. I wasn't prepared for what I was going to hear. I quickly made my way to the office and picked up the phone. "Is this Josif Wright?" the voice asked.

"Yes, it is," I replied.

"This is Brooke Hinson. I'm very sorry to bother you at work, but I can't wait any longer to tell you this. I have class with your son, Ryan. He's been confiding in me after class. If something doesn't change soon, Ryan might not live much longer."

I was stunned. Fear gripped my body. This fear was unlike any fear that I had ever experienced. *Oh, dear God!* I thought. Without hesitation, I asked the office aide if I could take the call in the counselor's office. Brooke said that she had class at the local junior college with Ryan and that they had become friends. Ryan confided in her for several weeks that he had been doing drugs and that he was afraid for his life. At that moment, all of my suspicions came to light. My mind went back to the two or three people who boldly and lovingly told me of Ryan's alleged drug use. I dismissed those accusations each time Ryan and I talked about it, mainly because he lied so well. There weren't glaring indications at that time, and any instances that would point to drug use were few and far between. He just didn't show a lot of the signs of drug use, and I didn't know what to look for. I thanked Brooke repeatedly and hung up the phone. I knew that she had saved my son's life with that phone call. I just sat there numb. I couldn't speak, couldn't cry, and couldn't process what I'd just heard.

Finally, I gathered enough strength to get up out of the chair. I knocked on the office door and motioned for the office aide to inform the principal that I had an emergency and I had to go home. I didn't know what to do and say to Ryan when I got home or how to handle this. "Give me wisdom," I whispered to God. I arrived at my dad's house where Ryan was. I told him that we needed to talk so we sat in his truck. I told him of my phone conversation with Brooke.

At first, he denied it, "No, that's not true! It's not true!" Ryan shouted. He started hitting the steering wheel with his fists until they almost bled. I tried to stop him. After I calmed him down, we talked for quite some time. Ryan finally confessed to becoming addicted to OxyContin and cocaine. He answered all of the questions I asked of him. Instead of months of lies and manipulation, he told the truth. He smiled and said, "It feels so good to get that weight off my shoulders."

Where do we go from here? I thought. "What do we do next?" I didn't have a clue. When I went home that evening, I told Bethany and Rebekah. They were devastated. I assured them that we would make it through all of this with God's help. What we didn't realize was that hell was just beginning for our family.

Ryan called me at school the next day. He and one of his friends wanted to talk to me. They came while I was watching my elementary school students on the playground. They said that they wanted to get off drugs. I shared with them how glad I was with their decision and had the opportunity to share the gospel with them before they left. *Man, I'm so glad that I caught this now*, I thought. *They can get treatment and get on with their lives.* But I had no clue about treatments. Did it mean going to rehab? Did Ryan need to go to a facility immediately so that professionals could help him? I was so ignorant and equally as naïve. Suboxone was starting to catch on in that area as a new drug to help addicts get off drugs. I didn't know what to do. I heard that Suboxone was a miracle drug but I wasn't sure that taking one drug to get off another drug was best. After praying about it and talking with Ryan and Bethany, we decided to see a doctor about getting a prescription for Suboxone. We thought that we would do the treatment and everything would get back to normal. Little did I know that Ryan's drug use to numb the pain of his childhood migraines and his grandmother's passing would intensify and not let up until at least 2014 when he went to rehab for the first time.

2

---•---

Why?

Everyone you meet is fighting some kind of battle.
Always be kind and compassionate.

There is a misconception that people have about those who become addicted to drugs. The addicts are thought of as terrible, reckless, uncaring, rebellious, and burdens on society. People think they are getting what they deserve when they're locked up in jail, develop a disease, become homeless, or die. More often than not, people who become addicted to drugs have tremendous ability and talents. They are people exactly like you and like me. Many people become addicted to drugs have done so as a result of an accident, surgery, or chronic pain. Money-hungry doctors have all too often shoved all kinds of medications in their faces so that they can make more money regardless of whether it makes people addicted to drugs, ruins lives, or even kill people. They are legalized drug dealers, and they write out prescriptions as fast as they can. Many of the addicts have made seriously bad decisions with who they hang out with or become close friends with. Maybe they lacked direction from a parent or guardian. Others turn to drugs to escape a terrible home life where chaos is the norm. Still others have someone very close to them dying. It can lead people to take drugs to make the pain go away for a while. Life can be difficult. Life can get complicated. If there isn't guidance, a healthy way to deal or cope with pain life can bring. Finding something to numb the pain sometimes becomes their option. Then once a person gets hooked, life becomes a war to stay clean.

There are four main reasons why Ryan got addicted to drugs: chronic pain, thoughts of feeling unloved, the death of his grandmama, and his rebellious nature. Ryan had chronic pain throughout his childhood and into his teen years. He was diagnosed with childhood migraines at the age of five. He didn't feel good most of the time. You would've never known it though. He excelled in the classroom and on the ball field. He never got into any kind of trouble at school throughout his elementary, middle school, or high school years. He did get into plenty of trouble at home though. He was very strong-willed and always had an edgy, rebellious nature. But from the outside looking in, we seemed like the perfect family with no glaring problems. I'm not one to be fake or phony. I would tell our children if we had a bad morning getting ready for school or church and someone asked how you're doing to say, "We had a bad morning." Now, obviously, we didn't go outside of our home and tell people that things were not good. We just dealt with it the best way we knew how. I would find out years later that Ryan did not love himself. I couldn't understand why because Bethany and I told him and Rebekah every single day that we loved them and that we would always be there for them. We didn't neglect them. We saw after their needs and wants. We celebrated birthdays, special occasions, and holidays with them. We started family traditions, and we read to them and prayed with them every day. But the enemy of our souls lied and set up fear and feelings of being unloved early in Ryan's life. For some reason, Ryan believed those lies. You see, the enemy doesn't just want to tell lies to people to keep them down for a short time. The enemy wants to set up a fortress with the lies he tells us when we're young. If a fortress of fear, self-loathing, hatred, anger, addiction, jealousy, etc., can be established at a young age, it will take an all-out war to tear those walls down. He continues to lie to us growing up, trying to eventually ruin our lives and keep us from fulfilling our God given purpose in this world. The enemy's ultimate goal is to steal, kill, and destroy. He is aided in accomplishing his goal by our turning from truth, going our own way, closely associating with people who aren't the best for us, looking for things in this world other than God to satisfy, etc. The enemy also wants us to turn our backs on God, be mad at Him, and blame Him for our health issues and personal issues.

The passing of my mom was when things really started going awry. She was his everything. He spent a lot of time with her and loved her dearly. She was the most nurturing, caring, and loving woman I've ever known. When Mama found out that she had cancer in April 2006, Ryan started reading his Bible more than any other time in his life. He took notes during church services and did devotions. When Mama passed away, Ryan felt as though God had let him down. In his mind, since he was reading his Bible and taking notes during church, God would somehow take her cancer away. He was angry at God for not sparing his grandmama, which he openly admitted to me later.

The last reason was simply Ryan's rebellious nature. He always tested the boundaries, not necessarily at school, but definitely at home. He would always run to the dark when he got into trouble at home. I never understood it. When things were not good at home because of a disagreement or because he had to be disciplined, he would gravitate to dark things. Eventually, each time Ryan would come back to me, crying and apologizing for disobeying or getting into trouble. We'd get things right, and the day would be much better. Later in his teenage years, if there was someone we thought he shouldn't hang around, he would find a way. For whatever reason, he gravitated to those people who don't fit the Christian youth mold. A person's close friend is one of the most important influences in anyone's life. Ryan's choice of close friends was usually not very good, especially throughout his senior year and after graduating.

3

———•———

Spiraling out of Control

In the multitudes of my anxieties within me,
Your comforts delight my soul.
—Psalm 94:19 (NKJV)

As I mentioned in chapter one, he was taking Suboxone as prescribed by a doctor in a neighboring county. Early on, it seemed as though the doctor didn't care about the patients that he prescribed Suboxone to. It seemed to me that he was in it to make more money. There was no talk of tapering down and coming off Suboxone completely within a year with counseling and support. We really weren't sure how long he should stay on this drug.

Even though things were out in the open about Ryan's drug use and we were actively seeking treatment through Suboxone, there wasn't a lot of peace in our lives. There would be days and even weeks of calmness in our home then arguments and battle of the wills would quickly take us back to an unpleasant place. Bethany and I constantly prayed for Ryan and Rebekah to desire to live godly lives. Looking back, I do believe that we pushed them too much at times, succumbing to the legalism that is so prevalent in some Christian circles. It made it much more difficult when Ryan would fill his mind with terrible music and media. He simply wasn't ready to give in to God. Our children didn't even want to go to church during this time.

It was difficult getting them up and ready on Sundays. I know this stemmed from the ugly experience that we had, leaving the church where I was the youth minister. It was still so fresh as it had happened several months earlier.

I was on staff there from January 2000 to August 2010, which is a long time to be a youth minister in one church. About midway through my tenure there, our church was searching for a pastor. We just had a wonderful interim pastor named Brother Johnnie. He mentored me and was so encouraging. He followed the Holy Spirit's guidance in leading the church and was straightforward and very matter-of-fact in dealing with people. He told it like it was. I admired that about him. Our church decided to call a man who had been in the Independent Baptist churches for nineteen years. He was what was known as an IFB (Independent Fundamentalist Baptist). In general, he was used to controlling all aspects of the independent churches he pastored, which was in stark contrast to the way a Southern Baptist church is governed. Southern Baptist churches work in an association and also in conjunction with a cooperative program of Southern Baptist churches as a whole to spread the gospel throughout their association, state, and world. Southern Baptist churches would be wise to only call Southern Baptist pastors. I wondered why this preacher spent time at churches for only four years or so. I know now.

This guy we called as pastor wanted to control our church by himself. He turned down good programs—such as : Royal Ambassadors, Girls in Action, Brotherhood, Women on Mission, etc.—and started programs that he was in favor of, none of which he followed through for any great length of time. He got angry when anyone questioned him and was one of most legalistic men that I have ever met. He had a big case of little man syndrome. I asked why he moved money from church account to church account, why he wanted to cut funding to missions, why he tried to block a youth mission trip, and why we were not meeting as a staff to pray, to name a few. He turned on me and tried to make me look bad in front of others, especially the deacon body. Church had become a war zone, and there were battles that were starting to be fought on a weekly basis. Another leader in the church told me to just do my job and keep quiet. But things were going on that were wrong, I couldn't just keep quiet. There's so much more to say about that church experience and the things he did before after I left, but I'll save that for another book. Eventually, he convinced the deacon body to dismiss me as youth minister for "not working with him," effective that day, August 22, 2010. No severance pay, no goodbyes to the youth, whom Bethany and I loved so dearly, no nothing. Gone from that church was youth witnessing at Walmart, weekly praying for a different nation, outreach to Hispanics, prayer breakfasts, and praying and witnessing to every person at the six or seven schools that our youth belonged to. It was over in one fell swoop. Instead of worship that night, the church leaders decided to discuss my being fired. Boy, did that ever backfire! People were up in arms about why I was being told to leave. Questions would be asked by church members, but valid answers would never come.

All of this didn't help the fact that Ryan was already living rebelliously, wanting to do his own thing. Up to that point, this war within the church was the biggest blow that our family had gone through. As far as that church goes, within a year and a half, over 150 people from this small church left. The preacher ended up having to leave that church a couple of years later. So if it took me being *kicked out* to expose him, so be it. He decimated this church, and it took a long time before things were relatively normal there again. This situation destroyed my children's trust in church leaders. It was a devastating blow to our family that we are still working through. You just don't expect lies, mistreatment, and a terrible lack of love to happen like that in a church setting. But sad to say, it happens all of the time. Bethany and I prayed for God to heal us and allow us to forgive. However, it has taken a long time for those things to happen. To this day, the legalism and judgment of this church and others like it have made my family cynical—especially Ryan and Rebekah—not readily trusting of people, let alone church leaders. We're trying to work through it with God's guidance.

Over the remainder of 2010 and halfway through 2011, I tried to remain optimistic, but things were by no means well with our family. Rebekah graduated high school in May of 2011 and was set to attend the University of Alabama on scholarship. Ryan finished his first year at a local junior college and was trying to decide what his next step was. As for me and Bethany, we were desperately looking for peace. We had forgotten what normal was. I guess we were experiencing a new normal now. It definitely wasn't the kind of normal that Bethany or I would have chosen for our family. There were several close calls during that period of time when things could have gone very bad. For legal reasons, I won't elaborate. The whole time, God had His hand upon us. He was molding us, building in us patience, and getting us mentally and physically tougher. In the coming months and years, we would need every single bit of that toughness and strength to keep moving forward and keep our sanity. It seemed that with each day, I increasingly got sick of this life and its problems, while Ryan and Rebekah grew increasingly cynical of church. I fervently prayed day after day for God to rescue us from all of this. I was just so numb to everything. I tried to read my Bible and pray. Many times, my prayer was simply, "God, please help." My mind would race wondering what had happened, how we got to that point, and what the next step was. I hated looking at myself in the mirror. It was just such a depressing time of uncertainty, doubt, and fear.

I tried to remain active, getting outside and exercising, but sometimes I just didn't have the desire to. I was a teacher and a coach at that time, so at least I was focusing on those things for most of the day. Mostly after practice or games and on weekends, I would sit in my backyard or drive up to our local park and just sit in silence. Other times, I'd sit in my office at home and beg God for miracles, sitting and listening to Laura Story songs and Casting Crowns songs like "Blessings," "What a Savior," "Prodigal Song," "If I Ever Needed You," "Always Enough," "At Your Feet," "Glorious Day," "To Know You," "Mercy," "Jesus Hold Me Now," and "Blessed Redeemer." I'd sit there for hours. "When are you going to intervene?" I would plead. "How long must we wait to see good days again?" I'd ask. It's strange that the times that I felt the most pain and agony were the times that I felt Jesus right there beside me. On some occasions, I would ask

God to put His arms around me and just hold me close. I felt Him so near. God touched me deep down in my battered and broken heart through those songs and many others. In the midst of deep and utter despair, I was experiencing "the peace that passes all understanding" that the Bible talks about in Philippians 4:7–8. God didn't take the pain away, but He comforted me in the midst of it. It was like I had been hit by a car and was in critical condition but someone *was* holding my hand, providing strength and encouragement. I grew up like Beaver Cleaver with few disagreements or fighting. My mom grew up hard, and she didn't want us to go through what she had been through. She was a happy person who loved life and people, and she was definitely loved by everyone who knew her. My dad was an associational missionary (home missionary). He had a very laid-back nature. This was the recipe for our happy Christian home. My parents loved the Lord and loved us children also. But the unrest in my home now was excruciating. I didn't feel that God had left me or my family, but I surely didn't know how to fight this except through prayer. Sitting in my office listening to music were very surreal yet precious times that I had alone with God in the midst of my pain.

During this time, Bethany and I lived in utter survival mode. We became paranoid when the phone would ring or when our text tones would go off. Whichever one of us answered the phone or text would give the other a thumbs-up sign if the other one walked into the room, signifying that it wasn't bad news or an urgent call. We lived in constant fear. Yes, we prayed and asked the Lord to calm our fears. We prayed that Ryan would be delivered and that he would surrender to God. It was just a fear that we constantly were asking God to help us with. Another thing we would do was refer to how we were doing in medical terms. If someone asked how things were going in our family, we would reply with the words *stable, serious, critical,* or, at times, *on life support.* That's just how we felt so that's how we answered. Sure, there were many, many days that we smiled and said we were doing fine. I think all humans say that or act like things are fine from time to time when things are falling apart. It comes fairly naturally when you don't want others to know your business. But this hospital terminology became the norm for us.

Bethany's brother and sister-in-law, Wayne and Leigh, agreed to let Ryan live with them in 2012 when he enrolled at a junior college in Birmingham, Alabama. Ryan was doing well so we thought that a change of scenery would be good. They loved him like their own but got more than they bargained for by letting him live there. I'm sure they learned a lot about parenting in dealing with Ryan living with them with his extremely strong-willed nature and sometimes sketchy actions and friends. Bethany and I were so grateful to them for allowing Ryan to live with them and give him a fresh start. As it turned out, Ryan wore out his welcome in a year's time after several incidents and was looking for another place to live. By the end of summer 2012, Ryan moved into Tracey Phillips' house in another part of Birmingham, Alabama. Tracey had her two children living with her and also another guy who needed a place to live. She is a precious angel in our eyes! She and her fiancé Jimmy were so good to Ryan, but they also held him accountable. Ryan definitely tested the waters, but they held his feet to the fire. Bethany and I will always cherish those two people for helping Ryan when he needed it. Ryan lived there for about a year while attending junior college and working at Subway. Ryan, as always, pushed the envelope at Tracey's house in different ways. He was very respectful of Tracey but also wasn't giving up on dabbling with drugs from time to time. She drug-tested Ryan on occasion and did not let him get away with anything. She and Jimmy loved Ryan like a son and treated him well. Tracey and Jimmy were to get married, and Ryan wanted to find an apartment and be out on his own. Things were still shaky with him though. We were apprehensive about him moving out of Tracey's house but knew that he needed to with the wedding coming up. Things were starting to erode in Ryan's life. He and his sister Rebekah had a falling out because of his behavior. Bethany and I could see him slipping into a dangerous lifestyle.

During these uncertain times, I would look forward to each evening at home. Even though I was having trouble sleeping at night, evenings had become my favorite time of the day. I think it was because I was at home and in a comfortable place where I didn't have to interact with anyone. My office, my bedroom, and my couch at 3:00 a.m. were safe places. They were places that I could read, pray, or just sit in bed, thankful that I had made it through another day. When I was finally tired enough, I could now go to sleep and forget about all of my problems. Of course those problems would immediately come to my mind as soon as I woke up the next morning, but at least there was a reprieve in not having to think about unpleasant things as I slept. I guess you could say that sleep was my drug, my escape from what was going on in my life and in the life of my family.

Many a night Bethany and I would cry ourselves to sleep, and I'm sorry to say that many times it was separately. An addiction like this can separate and isolate, tearing apart families and marriages. Oh, how it hurt my heart to hear Bethany on the other side of the bed silently whimpering as she tried to go to sleep. That hurt even worse. At times I would console her; other times I'd just pray for her silently. I will never forget each tear sliding down my face and hitting my pillow. Some nights I would clutch my small Gideon Bible and pray as I drifted off to sleep, oftentimes waking up several times during the night. Sometimes my hand would still be gripping that little Bible as hard as I was when I dozed off to sleep. It brought great comfort to me to hold that Bible next to my chest or hold it under my pillow. I felt that God was crying over Ryan's waywardness (as I was) and felt that He was even more near as I held that Bible. The Bible does say, "The Lord is near to the brokenhearted and saves the crushed in spirit" (Ps. 34:18, ESV). Other nights I just had to think back to happier times in my life. I would picture myself in the Dominican Republic, gazing at the beautiful green rolling hills. I've been to the country twice on mission trips, and I felt at home there. I would see myself at that little church in La Monteada where I first preached to Hispanic people with an interpreter and our youth group ministered to the people. It was a happy place that I loved, even though I had only actually spent one week there. The scenery was breathtaking, and it helped me to rest as I went there in my mind.

You see, addiction doesn't ease off or take a break because you have other things going on in your life. It's a 24-7 issue. Bethany and I still had our jobs to do. We were both teachers, and I was a varsity high school coach in several different sports. It was so difficult getting up and going to school to face students when I was dying inside. We fought that battle many mornings. If it weren't for God's grace and strength, there's absolutely no way that I could've made it. No way! Many days I would stare at our backyard through the window, praying that I could make it through the day so I could sit in that backyard in peace that afternoon. Many times at school, planning periods became times I could shut my office door, play soft music, and melt into my chair. God comforted me greatly during those times and gave me strength to keep going on. Those were extremely difficult days. The usual demands of the teaching profession coupled with demands of coaching two varsity sports was hard enough without throwing in horrific situations with your child. At times, it was unbearable. Looking back, I simply can't believe I did all that I did under the circumstances. Well, you do what you have to do at the time and trust God for help. He always provided all that I needed.

Things seemed okay for the next several months, then Ryan started dating this girl. Bethany and I were apprehensive about this relationship for several reasons. One reason was she had been involved with some things in the past. We knew someone who knew her closely, and that person warned us. Another reason for concern was the feeling we got when we talked to her and also what others close to her had said about her personally. We just felt strongly that Ryan and this girl didn't need to be around each other. This we knew. What we didn't know at the time was that this relationship would cause so much anxiety, grief, and pain.

Going through the roller-coaster ride of addiction, experiencing such legalism and ugliness in our church, and pretty much living with a permanent knot in my stomach caused by things that were happening in my family, I began to ask God questions. There were times when I would start to question the very faith that I held so dear for so many years. During the hunting season in the fall of 2012, I distinctly remember sitting in a small shooting house on a deer plot. The grass in the field was a beautiful green color. In the background was a gorgeous blue sky with a few puffy, white clouds placed in it. I looked to heaven and said, "God, I don't want to believe something just because my parents said it. I don't want to live in such a way because of any expectation on me by others. I want to hear from You directly. I want You to tell me truth and answer my questions. Let's start from the beginning. Are You there? I mean, is there a God?"

My question was immediately answered directly to my heart. Without a doubt, I heard Him say, "Yes, just look around you. The evidence is completely overwhelming."

I sat there for several hours, asking questions about life and listening for answers. Many questions were answered, such as, if the Bible was true, why was I here on earth, etc. Many questions were not answered, like how long would it be before life would be good again, when would this pain end, etc. I was assured that God loved me, had a plan to make my family whole again and reach hundreds of thousands with the Gospel of Jesus Christ. But I was going to have to wait. Ryan had to learn some things. Bethany and I were going to have to learn some things. I had to have complete and total faith, trust, and hope in God. It was going to be a long, hard, exhausting road, but He was going to make all things new in His time. I had no choice but to trust Him and fight through it. The Bible says in Isaiah 26:3 (ESV), "You will keep him in perfect peace, whose mind is stayed on you, because he trusts in you." Whenever you feel over-whelmed, totally stressed out, at your wit's end, or not sure what to do, refocus your mind. Talk to God out loud, ask Him questions, and tell Him all about your hurts, concerns, and desires. He knows them anyway, but there is just something about expressing those thoughts to the God of the universe that brings a sense of peace. Some of the peace comes from *getting those feelings talked out.* God may not answer right then, but deep thoughts that are not expressed verbally tend to eat away at us as we *hold them in.*

Another good way to feel peace is by focusing on something else, reading a book, or watching a documentary. I always found that it helped me to do something physical and to sweat, releasing endorphins. Playing basketball, jogging, or walking until I was tired helped me to keep my sanity during low times. You see, this addiction, this disease is all consuming. It completely takes over every area of your life. A person that's addicted becomes a liar and a master manipulator. They have to in order to continue their habit. No matter how much they love their family and friends, this disease will isolate them and drain them of health, strength, and identity until it sucks the very life out of its victim. It is no respecter of age, sex, color, social status, or talent. It rips relationships and families apart, leaving total devastation behind. It brings with it a depression, a dull, colorless existence that leads to a hatred for life, and an absence of happiness that destroys anything standing in its way of killing the victim and the victim's relationships. Its end is jail or death. It is incomprehensible, unexplainable, and horrific. You will begin to think that it has no end. Those are the exact times when you should get out of your house and exercise. You certainly don't want to risk slipping into depression by way of isolation. Depression and isolation can take the fight right out of you.

On one particular morning, I was very agitated over situations in our family. It was a very cloudy day, but there was no sign of rain. I was talking out loud, asking God why these things were happening. As I was about to turn onto the highway to head toward work, I asked God, "Do You really keep Your promises?" I looked up into this sky filled with clouds and saw a window cut perfectly out of the clouds. Inside the hole was a rainbow. I was so startled that I almost ran off the road. In the Bible, God put a rainbow in the sky as a promise. There was no reason for a rainbow to be in the sky. It hadn't rained nor was it going to rain that day. I was shaken back into reality. "Yes, You do keep Your promises. Thank you, God." These types of things happened to me and Bethany several times over those years. It showed me that no matter what happened, God was in control and that He would never leave us.

4

---•---

Search for Meaning

You will seek me and find me, when you seek me with all your heart.
—Jeremiah 29:13 (ESV)

The spring of 2013 saw Ryan excel academically in junior college. He was doing well in his classes and was working at Subway. Things were more stable, but then he started acting a little strange. My stomach was constantly tied in knots again. Then came the morning I received a text at school saying that Ryan had been arrested. He came home for the weekend and was heading back to Birmingham when the police picked him up after someone had called and told them that Ryan had drugs in his possession. He had to be at work in about four hours. What were we going to do? Would Ryan lose his job at Subway? I called Ryan's supervisor where he worked and told her what happened. She assured me that she would cover his shift. I tend to think that she wasn't very surprised at this turn of events.

At the time, the thought of him spending the night in jail was terrible, but that is what Bethany and I thought we needed to make him do. We prayed for his safety and tried to get some sleep. It was a very long night. The next day, my dad and father-in-law accompanied me to the county jail. We got a chance to talk to Ryan along with the sheriff. I simply can't describe the feeling I had sitting there with Ryan in a striped inmate uniform. It was almost more than I could bear. The sheriff talked sternly to Ryan, telling him that he had been watched for some time. I melted in my chair. Disappointment and embarrassment flooded my heart. Ryan was released to us, and we went home. I don't remember much of what was said the rest of the evening. I'm sure it was a quiet one.

Ryan seemed to have felt very badly about the way that he had been living and embarrassing his family by being locked up. He wrote me, Bethany, Rebekah, Nana, Pop, and my dad letters, expressing his sorrow. I prayed fervently for Ryan. I prayed that God would end this nightmare by having Ryan to make good decisions and to just *do right*. Many times while taking a shower, I'd bury my head in the bottom of the bathtub on my knees and cry out to God, begging Him to save Ryan's soul. I felt the most vulnerable in there, naked and having nothing to offer but my pleas for help. The rest of the spring, Ryan continued to work at Subway and finished his associate's degree in May. We were proud of his accomplishment, but he just seemed on edge the day of graduation. Even though things had been fairly stable since the arrest, there never seemed to be a lasting happiness with him. A few days of normality usually brought on speculation of wrongdoing, hanging around people that he shouldn't and arguing at home.

The summer of 2013 wasn't all bad. There were good times too. Things were becoming more stable. Bethany and I cautiously thanked God for that. All that summer, Ryan searched for truth. He was reading his Bible and going through Brian "Head" Welch's devotional, *Stronger: Forty Days of Metal and Spirituality*. It is, to this day, one of the best devotionals that I've ever read. Head Welch is very candid and straightforward in all of his books. He doesn't sugarcoat anything. Ryan wrote his thoughts and feelings in the margins in the pages of the book as he read each day. I could tell that God was speaking to him. I found out months and months later that Ryan contacted three friends from high school who were Christians that he had stopped hanging around. Ryan apologized to each one for leaving them and their friendships. Ryan was definitely seeking and trying to figure things out. But you know, before you get saved or changed by Jesus, you must know that you're lost.

After taking a summer class at the junior college in Birmingham and earning a second associate's degree in science (to go along with the general studies associate's degree he earned in May), Ryan decided that he wanted to go to the University of Alabama at Birmingham (UAB) to pursue a degree in dentistry or engineering. Bethany and I went with Ryan to orientation in July. The campus was beautiful, and we had good expectations for UAB. Hopefully this would be the new beginning that we were looking for. He was in the process of moving out of Tracey's house and into an apartment. He told me and Bethany that he had found an apartment. So a few weekends before school was to start, we went up, signed the lease, and he moved in. It was not in a great area but seemed to be okay. The guy across the hall from Ryan had lived there for thirteen years and assured us that he would look out for Ryan. Bethany and I were hoping that this move was going to be okay. Not long after moving in, Ryan told us that he felt very uneasy about being there so we figured that we should somehow break the lease and find another place. He came home the first weekend in August. Bethany, Ryan, and I talked for quite a long time. He opened up to us about a lot of things, things that left us very upset. He told us about his struggles from within. He also told us that he knew in his heart that he wasn't really saved and set free by God. It bothered us greatly but it also let us know exactly where he stood with the Lord. We knew that Ryan hadn't lived the type of life that would suggest that he was saved. I guess we held on to the fact that Ryan "prayed a prayer" when he was nine years old and was baptized. No one but God and the person truly knows if their heart and life has been changed by God through repentance. There were indications from time to time but not in the last few years. Nevertheless, we knew specifically what to pray for. We prayed that God would pursue Ryan with His grace and that it would be irresistible to him. As Ryan said goodbye and drove back to Birmingham, we prayed for safety. We were concerned about his mental state. Ryan was upset and depressed when he left. What a relief it was when Ryan texted that he made it back to his apartment. It was a bigger relief to hear that he went to work that next day. Two weekends later, we went up to stay with Ryan and had a good time. We could tell that he was glad we were there with him. When we left, Ryan texted and told us that he loved us and that he wished we would come back to visit soon. He would never really feel comfortable living in that apartment.

August 18, 2013, Ryan stayed up most all night with a shotgun by his bed. He must have believed that he heard things outside of his apartment. The sliding glass door lock that led to his balcony was broken and wouldn't fasten. He had to go to work the next day but was exhausted from staying up all night. On his way to work, he was involved in an accident that totaled his car. When the police came to investigate, Ryan was loud and belligerent. He was arrested for disorderly conduct the morning of August 19, 2013. Bethany and I were so disappointed. We decided to leave him in there two days before coming to get him out. Before being released, he would have to go before a judge. Bethany and I sat in the back of the courtroom, waiting for Ryan to get there. It was very frightening but we had to be strong for each other. Ryan entered the courtroom shackled to four other inmates. It was a traumatic experience for us all. The judge asked Ryan to stand and then talked directly to him. The judge then called me and Bethany to the front. It was very scary, but I could feel God was right there with us. The prosecuting lawyer and our lawyer conferred together with the judge. Ryan was to be placed on a probationary time, which he had to attend weekly meetings with Dr. Al for counseling. This would last from August to December. I don't think Ryan missed a single appointment. The thing that scared the crap out of me and Bethany was that in that whole experience, Ryan was not broken. He was still full of pride, and we knew exactly where pride leads to. It leads to a fall, and we just didn't know just how bad that fall would be.

Ryan rode home with me and Bethany after being released. On the way home, Ryan asked for Brother Ty's phone number. Ty was a trusted friend and pastor. I think I looked up Bro Ty's number in record time to give it to Ryan. I texted Ty and told him that Ryan wanted to call and speak with him. Ryan called and set up a time that next day to talk. I was fairly anxious, hoping that Ty would say something that would make Ryan to think deeply about his life and give his life to the Lord. Ryan texted me and told me that he and

Ty talked for about two hours and that it was very productive. The Lord led Ty to say something to Ryan that I believe was absolutely profound. He told Ryan to read James 1:5 and pray. It says, "If any of you lacks wisdom, let him ask of God, who gives to all liberally and without reproach, and it will be given to him" (Jas. 1.5, NKJV). Ty told Ryan that God wants us to ask for and then have wisdom. There's nothing more important in life that God wants us to have wisdom about than if we are truly saved or not. How profound! That is the very verse that I read and prayed for in the next several weeks for Ryan. I desperately wanted Ryan to repent and give his life to Jesus, but I knew that I couldn't push him. It had to happen in God's timing. It was very apparent that there was a war going on for Ryan's soul. The spiritual battle that Ryan was going through was so intense. The enemy wanted to destroy; God wanted to redeem.

5

Saved

*By an act of your will, you change your mind. By
an act of His will, He changes your heart.*

Bethany and I went back to Birmingham to visit Ryan the next weekend. He was to start school at UAB. We knew that we desperately
needed to find another apartment complex for him to live in that
was in a safer area. We looked at a lot of apartments that weekend
and really had a nice time visiting and talking with him. We talked
about all sorts of subjects. I don't quite remember how the topic of
salvation came up, but late Saturday night on August 24, we started
talking about it. Ryan listened with great attentiveness. I knew that
the Holy Spirit was speaking to Ryan's heart as we talked together.
He, Bethany, and I talked for quite a long while before going to sleep
at his apartment. The next morning after we awoke, Ryan said that
he wanted to call Brett and talk with him. Brett and Ryan played ball
and graduated together in high school. Brett gave his life to Jesus
earlier in the year and had really been living for the Lord in an out-
spoken way.

I knew that this was a crucial time in Ryan's life and that I
needed to text as many trusted people and ask them to pray for Ryan
to repent and be saved. So as Ryan called Brett and sat outside on
his balcony, I texted those trusted friends and asked them to pray

for Ryan's salvation. I then hurried to his bathroom, knelt on the floor, prayed as fervently as I ever had, and read scriptures dealing with salvation. Scriptures such as Psalm 40:1–3, Ezekiel 36:25–27, Romans 3:23–26, Romans 5:1–11, Romans 6:15–23, Romans 8:1–11, Romans 10:1–13, Ephesians 2:1–10, and 2 Corinthians 5:12–21. Many other scriptures were read while I was in the bathroom. It seemed like I was in there for a very long time. There was a tremendous spiritual battle taking place for my son's soul, and I was going to fight tooth and nail. I knew that the enemy wasn't going to give up. I also knew that the enemy was no match for the scriptures and for the fervent prayers people offered on Ryan's behalf. I prayed with conviction, passion, and boldness for the God of the universe to hear and to call Ryan to repentance in an irresistible way. But Ryan had to make that choice to repent and trust in Jesus. This was all-out war!

After about thirty minutes, I heard the glass door to the balcony slide open. I scrambled to my feet and opened the bathroom door. Bethany, who had been praying beside the bed, stood up and looked toward the balcony. Ryan entered through the door and I'll never forget the look on his face. He had the most peaceful, relieved look on his face. He didn't have to say a word. His face said it all. "Praise Jesus!" Bethany and I said as we ran over to embrace our son.

Tears streamed down Ryan's face as we held him ever so tightly. It was a very sweet time together. Ryan had finally repented. Jesus had saved my son! What a great day August 25, 2013 was! I can still remember Ryan talking on his phone as we went to get something to eat. "I got saved!" he would tell one person after another. Two of the best days of my life were when my children, Rebekah and Ryan, repented of their sins and trusted in Jesus to save them. It is very important to remember that when someone truly gets saved, the enemy will try to get them off track. He can't take salvation away from the true Christian but can try to entice them away from living for the Lord. The enemy loves to try to make Christian people useless in any way that he can. Ryan found a new apartment, was reading his Bible each day, started attending The Church at Brook Hills, and was really growing in his new faith. He deleted his old friends out of his phone within the week. He told me that he was a new person and that he was learning so much in his daily Bible reading time. Bethany and I thanked God every day for saving Ryan's soul. It wasn't surprising that the enemy came at Ryan with temptations a few months later.

The girl Ryan dated six months ago just so happened to have enrolled at UAB, and they bumped into each other one day. If only Ryan walked the other way. If only Ryan had not stopped to talk to her. If only he ran in the opposite direction. If only, if only, if only. The decision to renew this relationship was a terrible one and eventually lead to more heartache than our family thought we could ever endure. (Some decisions we make can literally ruin our lives. This was one such decision for Ryan). So Ryan let his guard down and hooked up with this girl again. It's not surprising that within three months, cocaine, pills, and alcohol were again a part of their relationship. Once the enemy gains a foothold, anything can happen. They spent a lot of time together doing drugs and missing class, among other things. When Bethany and I found out that this girl was back in the picture, we were devastated. What were we going to do? At the time, we didn't know about the drugs that they were doing, only that they were not good for each other. Ryan continued working at Subway and going to school, but it was very evident to his boss, teachers, and classmates that things were not good with him. To us, living three hours away, there were not glaring symptoms that all was not well. Bethany and I were teaching school and coaching volleyball at our high school so we were pretty busy. Rebekah knew more of what was going on than we did but wouldn't say anything to us. She was trying to protect us from all of the heartbreak she knew we would have when we heard, but it was killing her inside to know these things about Ryan.

Sometime early into 2014, Ryan used heroin for the first time. I know how it came to be and who supplied it but can't reveal the specifics at this time. As he would later tell me, this would be one of the worst decisions of Ryan's life. After taking heroin, a person's body screams for more. If it's not taken again, withdrawals will happen several hours later. Withdrawals are what many have experienced as some of the worst bodily experiences that they've ever felt. This is what people who have become addicted experience over and over again unless they take the drug into their body every so often. The addiction snowballs until, eventually, the addicted person has to have more and more, usually leading to needing it every day and several times a day. If the person doesn't die, they eventually pursue nothing in life but that drug. It becomes an obsession. It strips away their very identity and can cause all kinds of health, mental, family, relational, and legal issues.

To me and Bethany, things seemed okay with Ryan and this girl as we got into the spring of 2014. The crazy thing was that they were reading the Bible and devotionals together all while doing drugs. I haven't quite figured out the rationale behind that yet. I guess it was the spiritual pull from God to get clean along with the mental, physical, and emotional pull of the heroin. But with drugs, if an abuser lives long enough, there will be a day of decision. As it turned out, thankfully, that day would come very soon for Ryan.

6

Shattered

Be pleased, O Lord, to deliver me; Oh Lord, make haste to help me.
—Psalm 40:13

As the spring went along, Bethany and I felt that something was terribly wrong. For the first time in his life, Ryan's grades started dropping. He would have other people at Subway cover for him and things just seemed like they were not going well with him. We kept in contact with him through texts and phone calls, but some of the texts late at night were very long and some of them were strange-sounding. We had hoped that Ryan was doing what he was supposed to be doing but Bethany and I both could feel the Holy Spirit telling us that things were not good throughout the spring of 2014.

In late May 2014, Ryan came home for the weekend. He was very quiet. There was an odd feeling in the house. Things just didn't seem okay. He walked around the yard and sat in a chair in the backyard. He was definitely in deep thought. I went out back to sit with him. I could tell that something was very wrong and that there was something that he wanted to say. In the next few minutes of conversation, Ryan would tell me what had been going on. To say that I was not prepared for his confession would be a tremendous understatement. We talked for a few minutes and then he confessed that he had become addicted to heroin. The girl he was dating had gotten heroin from her dealer and brought it to Ryan to try several months earlier. He said that he wanted to tell us many times that he was addicted but just couldn't.

Oh, dear God! I thought to myself. I knew heroin was bad but I had no clue just how bad this was. There on his arms were track marks that I had only heard of or seen in pictures of addicts. It was like it wasn't even real. I guess I was in shock. I told him that we would get him help and that it was going to be okay. I assured him that his family would be there for him. As I went inside to gather Bethany and my daughter Rebekah in my bedroom to tell them, my mind raced. *How in the world do I tell them that Ryan is addicted and needs treatment? How?*

I had to remain calm even though it felt like I had been shot in the stomach with a shotgun. In addition to being calm, I had to assure them that we would seek treatment and that the God of the universe would be with us to guide us and take care of us. I know that Bethany and Rebekah cried. I don't recall crying. Remember, I had to be calm, strong, and courageous. I had to exude positivity in God taking care of the situation. He had to go back to school to finish the last week or so. I didn't know what to do after that. I had no dealings with anything like this. I talked with Nana about researching detox and rehab facilities so we could get him to one soon.

Ryan went back to school, and within a week or so, he would be finished with the semester. During that time, Nana and I frantically researched facilities all across the United States. We prayed fervently for God to lead, guide, and direct us to the one where Ryan needed to be. It was a daunting task for two people who had no clue where to go or even what to look for in a rehab facility. The thing that we both agreed on was that the facility that we eventually would choose needed to be faith-based. Nana and I searched the Internet for hours upon hours, made phone calls, and prayed that God would lead us to the right place. We narrowed it down to two rehabilitation centers. One was very expensive and didn't have many people on staff that had been recovering addicts. It was in Florida. The other was the House of Hope (HOH) in Adelanto, California. I was starting to get really stressed out because I just didn't know which rehab to choose. I liked the fact that most of the people on staff at HOH could identify with Ryan because they had gone through difficult times of addiction themselves or had addiction issues in their families. After extensive research of HOH, it seemed that they really cared for the people who came in and wanted to see lives changed by introducing them to Jesus. I also liked the daily schedule that HOH put together. The more I visited their website, the stronger I felt that HOH was the place Ryan needed. But time was getting short. By what Ryan was saying on the phone, we needed to get him to a detox and then to a rehab soon. We prayed fervently for wisdom, guidance, and direction. One night while flipping through the channels on TV, I came upon four consecutive shows that either had *hope* in the title, a character named Hope in the program, or had the word *hope* on the glass door in the show. *Wow, that's it!* I thought. I knew beyond a doubt that God was telling me where I should send Ryan. I called Mary Louise Fiddler who was helping us secure a bed at HOH. She and her husband, Rick Fiddler, were the founders of House of Hope. She said that God had impressed upon her that Ryan needed to come so she assured me that she would save a bed for him. "Thank you, God" I said under my breath, feeling relieved. So the plan was to get Ryan to detox and from there we would fly to California and get him to HOH.

The week that followed would be horrific. Ryan came home after taking his finals at college but was starting to feel bad from withdrawals that were coming on. We went took him to a hospital outside of the county that evening. Ryan told the doctor what was going on. They happened to have a detox at that particular hospital so we decided to take him there the next day. I'll never forget paying $3,500 for detox and then watching them take him away from us down the hallway and into the elevator. "We'll take care of him," the lady said.

Bethany and I drove home, barely saying a word to each other. Ryan was able to call us each evening to talk for a very short period of time. I remember distinctly what Ryan said after the second day at the hospital detox. He said, "Daddy, this is not the place."

My heart sank. I thought that he was telling me that just because he didn't want to go through with the detox. He asked me to come get him, but I didn't. He needed to get through the detox process. Ryan didn't call for two days. I was a little relieved about not getting a call on day three because it was just so painful to speak with him in that situation. When I didn't get a call on day four, I decided to call the detox facility. Much to my horror, they told me that someone came and picked him up the night before. It turned out to be his girlfriend. Ryan had called her and asked her to pick him up. She did just that and took him back to her apartment in Birmingham. I immediately called Ryan's cell phone and talked briefly to him. He said that the detox facility was corrupt and that there were so many people in there just to get contacts for more drug use. One of the drug suppliers he knew even worked at that hospital. I guess I was so naïve and clueless that those things didn't even cross my mind. It angers me to this day.

He told me where he was, and in the middle of the conversation, he said, "I gotta go." Then he hung up. Frantically, I called back a few times. I couldn't get in touch with him so I decided to race to Birmingham, not really knowing what I'd find when I got there. I got halfway to Birmingham (150 miles) when I got a call from someone who was there with Ryan and his girlfriend. They said that a scary situation happened there and gave me the address to her apartment. Her apartment was gated and in the middle of a subdivision. Even though I had the address, it was difficult actually getting into the complex. Adrenaline poured into my bloodstream. I was going around in circles in this subdivision, and my phone was about to die. I was losing time. Frantic and screaming for the Lord to help, I then saw the entrance to the complex. The gate was open. I drove in and ran up the stairs to the apartment. Thank God Ryan and his girlfriend were okay. They had a big scare that could've ended badly. After talking and sorting things out for a few hours with the people there, Ryan and I decided to go talk with his counselor, Dr. Ted. Dr. Ted had been so good to Ryan and had counseled with him for about a year or so. My brother-in-law, Wayne, met us at Dr. Ted's office where we talked for a long while. It was there that we got on the phone with Mary Louise Fiddler at the House of Hope. There was a brief time in Ryan's conversation with Mary Louise that we thought he may back out. She was kind yet matter-of-fact with Ryan. I begged for God to work it out. Finally, he said he would go. We just needed plane tickets. We went back to Ryan's apartment where I tried to get him to go to sleep so I could call and get a flight out the next day. He was very fidgety and wouldn't be still. He walked outside, and I couldn't find him. "God, please help me to get him back inside and asleep," I prayed.

A neighbor walked over to me and told me which apartment he went in. I went over and told him to come back over to his apartment now so we could get some sleep. I finally got him back in his apartment. He laid down to sleep about 12:30 a.m. I didn't have a computer. All I had was my iPhone to try to get a flight out the next morning. I looked and looked through flights to find one that would fly us into Ontario International Airport in Ontario, California. After about forty-five minutes of looking for a flight, I found one in first class. It was all I could find. It was going to be over a thousand dollar per ticket, but I didn't care. I had to get him to California so I booked the flight.

A little bit of time went by, I got to thinking that the flight itinerary should be confirmed in my e-mails. It wasn't there! Maybe I didn't wait long enough. I thought it would show up instantly. Why isn't it showing up? I asked myself these questions and many more. I had to have conformation. I don't care if I buy two separate flights to California. I've got to make certain that we have tickets. So I got back on my iPhone and looked for flights again. I looked through every airline that there was. I was starting to get really tired. My eyes were blurry. The iPhone screen was small so I constantly had to widen the screen to see it better. All I could think about was, *In about ten to twelve hours, Ryan would be in the withdrawals. God, you've got to do something!* I was so upset, almost crying. I searched for what seemed like hours before coming across a perfect flight itinerary. *How could I have not seen this one before?* I thought. I knew I had looked through all of them. Nevertheless, God led me to this flight. I quickly bought two tickets for Ontario, California, on Southwest Airlines for June

19, 2014. We would be leaving at 10:35 a.m. from Birmingham, Alabama. After one plane change in Las Vegas, Nevada, we would arrive in California at 7:00 p.m. that night. I checked my e-mails. "Thank you, God!" It showed up! Just to be sure, I called Southwest and asked if they would verify the itinerary. They did. Oh, Lord, what a relief! I don't know how in the world the first purchase didn't go through but thank God it didn't. I was absolutely exhausted, mentally and physically. I still needed to pack for Ryan's forty-day stay at HOH. I packed as best I knew how, moved the recliner in front of the door, and plopped down. I asked the Lord to help me sleep and also asked that God would have Ryan get up and get on the flight with no problems. Before drifting off to sleep, I asked God for strength for what would be an extremely long day of traveling. I did get to sleep but it was a short night.

7

House of Hope

*Joy does not always have to be present in happiness
nor does it have to be absent in despair.*

Early the next morning, Bethany called several hours before we were
to be at the airport. She and her mom were heading to the apartment
to drive us to the airport. I was so thankful for that. At least I would
have a small amount of time to rest before getting on the plane. Ryan
got right up, had a shower, and got dressed. Thank God. Bethany
and Nana arrived at Ryan's apartment and shortly after we left for
the airport. After arriving at the airport, we said our goodbyes to
Bethany and Nana and prepared to check in. Secretly, I was terrified
that somehow there could be heroin residue inside any of the bags I
packed for Ryan. If something like that was found in our bags at an
airport, it would be bad—real bad. Cold chills went up my back as
we had our bags checked. On the outside I appeared calm, but inside
I was raging. It was such a sigh of relief to get past each bag check
station. I guess the paranoia of watching too many episodes of the
Locked Up Abroad series didn't help me mentally. After boarding the
plane, I was thankful that we had made it to another checkpoint on
our way to House of Hope.

We had good flights to Las Vegas, Nevada, and again to Ontario,
California. It was amazing to see the people God had ordained us to

sit by. My seat was behind Ryan's seat on both flights. Ryan sat beside a married couple he talked with the entire flight to Las Vegas. They were godly people that were probably in their early forties. They were so kind to Ryan. He told them of his struggles and where he was going. At the end of the flight, the lady hugged Ryan and told him that she would be praying for him. She was so sincere. After changing planes in Las Vegas, we boarded the next plane for California. During that flight, Ryan sat beside a Hispanic man probably in his early fifties. He and Ryan talked a lot during the flight. When we all got off the plane, the gentleman had tears in his eyes when he told Ryan that his brother died of a heroin overdose. Before saying goodbye, he told Ryan to rely on the Lord and don't give in. I was thankful for the divine meetings Ryan had on those two flights.

We went by the rent a car station to get a car to drive to HOH. Avis had no cars left. Hertz had no cars left. Enterprise had no cars left. There was one more car agency still open. "Please, God, I'm getting worried. Help us!" was all I could say as I tried not to let Ryan know that I was getting worried. They had one car left. *Thank you*, I thought with a great sense of relief. Ryan and I rented a car and after a quick call to Mary Louise we headed toward House of Hope in Adelanto. The traffic was terrible, but we were on our way. Ryan slept in the passenger side while I drove. I was in no rush. I wouldn't risk going too fast. We drove about fifty miles and arrived at House of Hope in the high desert. "Dear God, thank you," I whispered as I parked. I awakened Ryan and we got out of the car.

Two guys that were in the HOH program came toward us as we got out of the car. One of them asked Ryan, "Are you the new guy? We're glad to have you."

That comment made us feel better. We went to front door. Mary Louise greeted us. She was so warm and kind. There was such a sweet presence in that place that was very inviting, loving, and comforting. I could just feel the presence of the Holy Spirit there among us. *This is the place*, I thought. We met most of the guys living there. They were all such sharp-looking guys. They just needed help. After being shown around the property, oriented to different rules and procedures, and having all of Ryan's bags checked, it was time to say goodbye. The intake guy told me that for Ryan's sake, I didn't need to have a long, drawn-out goodbye. I agreed. This was so difficult for me because I enjoyed loving on my children as they grew up. I hugged and kissed them probably more than most dads. My mom was a hugger and she definitely passed that down to me. I loved them very much. I thought back to those many seasons that I played adult baseball and roller hockey in Alabama. I skipped several games just to spend more time with them. But this was different. I needed to leave and let the healing begin. We had traveled over two thousand miles to get Ryan help at a place God led us to. It was time to go. Ryan came over and I told him that God would take care of him and that everything was going to be ok. I hugged and kissed him and hurried out.

I sat in the car for several minutes, trying to take in all that had happened to get us to California. As I drove away from HOH, I thanked God over and over for His guidance and protection. I asked Him to heal Ryan and make him whole again. I spent the first part of the night sleeping in the car in a Subway parking lot. From there, I went back to the rental car center at the airport to turn the car back in. My return flight was scheduled for 10:20 a.m. I was exhausted and wanted to get some sleep. It was a little after midnight at that point. The airport bus driver told me that it would be better for me to sleep in that meeting room in the rent-a-car place near the airport because the airport would be so bright with all of the lights on. So I sat on the floor by the plug for about twenty minutes to charge my phone before going in the meeting room to try to sleep. The only comfortable position I could get in was just laying my head on the table while sitting in the chair. I slept off and on for an hour or two before a security guard knocked on the outside window and motioned for me to get out of the room. I spent the next couple of hours trying to sleep in a chair in the rent-a-center lobby. The lights inside the lobby were very bright, and I was so cold. I hadn't shaved in several days, only had that one beige rolling bag, and was wearing a gray hoodie. I noticed a few times the security guard coming into the lobby and sitting directly across from me to keep an eye on me. I either looked suspicious or he thought I was homeless. I awoke again about 5:00 a.m. and decided that I would go catch a bus to the airport. It appeared that the well-dressed people getting on the bus were looking down on me. I wish I could've heard their thoughts. That certainly gave me a new perspective on how we oftentimes judge others by appearance, which is so unfair.

After about a week, Ryan could have five-minute calls in the evenings. I cherished those phone calls. God was opening his eyes through the renewing of his mind. In those phone calls throughout the forty days, Ryan told me that he had not been sorry until now that his words had been cheap in the past and that he was sick and tired of his way. He said that drugs messed the wires up in his brain and warped his mind, making him an angry person and someone that had lost who he was. Ryan also told me that there were many people he needed to make amends with. I was so thankful that God was moving in his life. Ryan was taking responsibility for his actions and growing in the Lord. We prayed each day for his recovery and for the staff at HOH that were leading him. During the forty days at House of Hope, they fed the homeless, spent a day at the San Diego beach, took part in group and individual counseling sessions, and attended church on Wednesdays and Sundays. Starting and ending each day with the Word was a big part of their program as well as taking part in certain Bible studies. I was so thankful for the HOH staff praying with and counseling with these guys who had been caught in the snare of addiction. Ryan was going through the program and getting close to graduating from HOH. Bethany and I knew that he had to come home but we wondered if forty days being there was really enough time. The evening of Ryan's graduation, Mary Louise made sure that we were able to listen in on Ryan's graduation via conference call. I thanked the HOH staff for all that they did for Ryan. The HOH staff said that they believed that Ryan would do great things for the Lord.

One of the things that drew me to the House of Hope in the first place was the main scripture verse on their website. It resonated with me. It was Isaiah 61:1, the prophecy that Jesus would proclaim while on earth some six hundred years later in Luke 4:18. It says, "The Spirit of the Lord is upon Me, Because He has anointed Me to preach gospel to the poor; He has sent Me to heal the broken-hearted, To proclaim liberty to the captives, And recovery of sight to the blind" (Lk. 4:18, NKJV). Those verses actually go on to say that Jesus Himself will give beauty for ashes, oil of joy for mourning, and a garment of praise for the spirit of heaviness. I really believed that Ryan would be used by God in the future to heal the brokenhearted by proclaiming liberty to people that were held prisoner by addiction or financial situations.

Several other people spoke at Ryan's graduation before Ryan himself spoke. Ryan thanked the HOH staff and told them that he loved them. He said that he arrived at HOH with no hope, only focused on himself, and it was killing him and his family. He went on to say that he had grown up a lot there and learned to listen to what God was leading him to do. He finished by saying that "It's not how you start, it's how you finish." He expressed interest in opening up his own rehab in the future to help those caught in addiction. To hear Ryan speak and give God the glory and honor made our hearts sing. It was such a refreshing experience, listening to all that God was doing in Ryan's life. Now came the real test, coming home away from that *controlled* environment.

Our volleyball team had a summer game on Monday, July 28. As soon as the game was over, I drove up to Birmingham to pick Ryan up from the airport. His plane was to land at 6:00 p.m. As I made the trip to Birmingham, it was hard to contain my anxiousness. Then something very strange happened as I was driving through the airport. As I was nearing the parking deck, I looked to my right. A beautiful dove came out of nowhere and flew right next to my truck for about five seconds. It veered off as I got to where I was going to turn. I had such a feeling of peace seeing that dove, and I knew that God sent that dove directly to me as visible sign of hope. After parking, I googled doves and found that hope, faith, and peace were what doves symbolized. I thanked God for sending this incredible sign and quickly walked toward the airport entrance. I arrived at the airport an hour or so before Ryan's plane was to arrive. I couldn't wait to see him. The talks we had over the last couple of months on the phone while he was in California had become progressively more encouraging. He was reading his Bible each morning, attending counseling sessions and group sessions several times a day, and seemed to be maturing as a young man. Bethany and I were so thankful for the growth that was taking place in his life. We were really hoping that he had detached from the girl that he had been seeing also. She wasn't good for him, and he wasn't good for her. Bethany and I were still apprehensive about his return after the traumatic events that had led him to detox and rehab. We just didn't know what to do. By all indications, he had improved tremendously and was ready to return. I guess we thought that forty days of clean time in a godly environment was going to "cure" him. Looking back, it would've been much better to have stayed six to nine months. Long-term help and accountability are definitely best. But you know what they say about hindsight.

I paced around the airport, looking at the arrival schedule of his plane. Finally, it was time. I stood there near the terminal, anxiously waiting for the plane to land. The arrival status showed "arrived." I felt like the prodigal son's father, just waiting to see him and run to hug him. The people started coming out of the terminal. *Oh Lord, when will I see him?* I thought. I was so anxious. Then I saw him at last. He looked so healthy, so alive. Our eyes met, and all I could see was that beautiful trademark smile of his. "Thank God," I said. I moved quickly toward him, and we embraced. I wanted to cry as I told him that I loved him. We headed to baggage claim to get his bags then to his apartment for a few days. I got a guy's number who helped addicts. His name was Tim. He told me that a guy named Rock, the founder of a recovery ministry in Birmingham, met with different recovery groups each week. Ryan and I went to talk with Rock and ended up staying for a meeting. There we met two guys, Eric Thomas and Keith Russell, who would become good friends and helped Ryan tremendously in the future. They would become such a blessing in our lives.

The next morning for me and Ryan was one that I will never forget. Ryan asked if we could get up early and go fishing at the pond at his uncle's farm. I agreed. We got up early and headed to the farm. The morning was beautiful! God painted a beautiful sky for us as we fished. We had such a good time together. It had been so long since I felt happiness and joy. I thanked God for the experience. In a few days, Ryan and I went home to see Bethany and Rebekah.

8

Shattered Again

God gives you just what you need when you need it most.

After spending several days at home, Ryan was going to go back to Birmingham, find a sponsor to help encourage him, go to Narcotics Anonymous (NA) meetings and get back in school. Things were looking good until Ryan got on his cousin's dirt bike. Ryan had only been back from California six days when he broke his foot in eight places on that stupid bike! *Are you serious?* I thought to myself. He, his uncle Wayne, and cousin had taken turns driving it around and jumping over the dirt road. Then on probably the last dirt-bike ride of Ryan's life, he lost control after the jump and crashed badly. Wayne said that it really could've been more serious than it actually was. He thought Ryan could've been killed. Lord, why did they have to get on a dirt bike? There was no reason. Well, now school was out of the question until at least January, and he would have to take pain medication to help deal with the broken foot. What a terrible, terrible happening.

Ryan found a sponsor who checked up on him as he attended NA meetings each week. I don't how much good it really did. Ryan was getting depressed and started spending more and more time alone in his apartment. Alone, that is, until he and that girl hooked up again. Somewhere along the way, Ryan started using heroin again. One of the counselors at the outpatient program Ryan was taking part in called me at school one day in October and told me that Ryan was in danger and needed help. Yet another person saved Ryan's life with a phone call. I immediately called Ryan, and he confessed.

Oh God in the depths. In need of miracles! 10-31-14 5:55am
Make haste to save, heal, redeem. Once and for all.
Power of Almighty God. Break chains. Hurry.
Solid ground. Only in + through Christ!

Friends, Keith and Eric, went to Ryan's apartment, talked to him, and stayed with him, helping him deal with this relapse. Ryan was going to try to detox at his apartment, which made us all very nervous. It turned out that it was much too painful to attempt so Eric drove Ryan to Bradford Health Services in Warrior, Alabama. He and Keith were able to get Ryan in that day. I drove up and met Eric there as Ryan waited to be checked in. Ryan spent November 2 to 17 there, detoxing and then going through individual and group counseling. There's no doubt that Keith and Eric saved Ryan's life. For that, I am eternally thankful. We picked Ryan up November 17 and headed back home. We actually had a good Thanksgiving a few weeks later and had Christmas together as a family to finish the year out. Year 2014 was an extremely difficult, gut-wrenching year. July and December were the only good months. I was so glad that year was about to end. "Thank you, Lord, for getting us through the year. Please, God, please let 2015 be better," I prayed.

Ryan just couldn't stay clean. Spending time with that girl we knew wasn't good for him, being depressed at times, and just not hanging around people who wanted to be clean were constant issues. There were warning signs in late January 2015. It all came to a head on February 1. Ryan was so in a hurry to get back to Birmingham from his Nana and Pops that day. After being pressured, Ryan said that the reason he wanted to go back to Birmingham was to do heroin, simple as that. We went through a terrible ordeal that morning trying to handle the situation. It was the worst day of our lives up to that point. Finally, the probate judge told us of a detox in Troy, Alabama, called The Journey. She knew the owner, and we talked to him on the phone. Ryan said he would probably go there or back to a detox, but he needed to get to Birmingham first. Ryan, Nana and I got in my truck and went to Birmingham. We waited for a day in a half, trying to get an opening at a detox facility above Birmingham, Alabama. February 2, I called the facility many times, asking about an opening. Even though they were expecting an opening soon, it just wasn't working out. Nana and I agonized day and night waiting for them to let us know something. That evening, I felt that I needed to reach out to Don Wheat, the program supervisor at The Journey. Don said that he had an opening for us so we could bring Ryan there the next day. "Praise God, we're going to Troy," I told Nana. Ryan agreed that he needed to detox at The Journey and then go to Turning Point in Thorsby, Alabama. I heard about it being a great place to recover. Ryan even told me earlier that as he was looking through some of his old things and came across notes from a sermon he had taken. It was from David Jeremiah's *Turning Point* TV program in California. The name *Turning Point* just jumped out at us. *That's got to be a sign*, we thought. I spent the entire night on the couch, holding Ryan's legs and rubbing his feet. His legs and body jerked throughout the night from spasms as a result of the withdrawal. I prayed over and over for God to rescue him from this disease.

The next day, February 3, we made the trip to Troy. Ryan got checked in. It was difficult leaving him there but we knew it was best. He was in God's hands. While Ryan was in The Journey detoxing and going through the program, we prayed with passion and fervor.

We prayed for healing, grace, and mercy from God. I called Chris who was the intake guy at Turning Point, a faith-based rehabilitation facility about two and a half hours from where I lived. I researched Turning Point on the Internet and prayed about what to do. I felt that this was the place he needed to go. Chris and I talked about Ryan being discharged from The Journey on February 9 and going directly to Turning Point in Thorsby, Alabama. Everything was set. February 7 around 9:00 a.m., Don called. He said that Ryan wanted to leave detox. I was speechless. The relief knowing that Ryan was getting help had turned to sorrow in an instant. I didn't know what to do so I went to the woods, a place of comfort to me. There I sat beside a tree for over four hours, thinking, praying, and pleading to God to give me wisdom and also help Ryan. While I was sitting in the woods, I wrote a long poem. Sometimes in the midst of turmoil and pain, it helps to pour out your soul through journaling and writing poems. As I came to the last line in the poem, I sat for more than fifteen minutes trying to come up with the words. I felt God tell me, "Let Me handle this. Give it to Me, and I'll finish the last line." I agreed to let God handle it.

Almost instantly, Don texted me. He told me that Ryan promised to finish the detox program. Seconds later, God gave me the words to the last line of the poem. Later that evening, I texted Don. He told me that Ryan was participating and interacting with other patients in the program. He went on to say that Ryan had settled down. I was so thankful. But things would end up taking a drastic turn. Two days later while I was at school, Don texted, "Call me, it's important." I had a terrible feeling in the pit of my stomach. This was the day Ryan was supposed to complete the detox program there and head to Turning Point. I got a teacher to watch my class and hurried outside to call. Don told me that Ryan wanted to talk to me. My stomach started to tighten even more.

"Dad, I just want to tell you that I'm not going to Turning Point right now," he said. "To be honest, I'm just not ready to submit to God." Total devastation.

I went to the school office to my principal, Mr. Jackson. He was so supportive and so kind. I asked him if I come go home. He said yes. I thanked God for his encouragement and understanding. The next few days were kind of a blur. Bethany and I prayed for Ryan's return, not really knowing how long it would be before we saw him. Again, the Lord filled us with peace, even though our hearts were shattered.

For two days, we didn't know where Ryan was. He simply texted us and said that he was safe. I'm thankful that Ryan stayed in contact those two days with our friend Connie, my sisters Elizabeth and Lynn, and Heath, the guy who was to marry my niece Brianna. Our hearts broke those two nights. Evidently, during the second evening, something very scary happened where Ryan was staying. I don't know what happened but I'm glad that it did. He called and asked Heath to pick him up late that night, which he did. Heath also convinced Ryan to go to Turning Point the next day. That was a pivotal moment in Ryan's life and quite possibly saved his life. We all felt so much better knowing that Ryan was at Heath's house that night. "Thank you for keeping Ryan alive, Lord," Bethany and I prayed. We thanked Heath for allowing God to work through him to get help for Ryan.

Early the next morning, I sent my friend Mark Cahill an e-mail, explaining the situation. I tried to keep in contact with Mark and keep him updated not only on Ryan's difficulties, but also his progress. Mark was actually the first person that I talked to about Ryan back in 2010. Mark, as always, had great advice. He said that in a hundred years, it wouldn't matter that Ryan became addicted to drugs. It would only matter that he surrendered to Christ, made a difference in people's lives, and fulfilled his purpose on earth. I'll never forget that conversation. While e-mailing Mark, he quickly replied and said to get Ryan in the car and take him to Turning Point before he changes his mind. As I was e-mailing Mark, Ryan actually drove up the driveway to our house. I quickly finished my e-mail to Mark, and we both got ready to leave. Heath pulled up not long after Ryan got there so we got Ryan's things in his vehicle and headed to Thorsby, Alabama on February 11, 2015.

9

———•———

Turning Point

When you're broken within, be willing to change
then the healing can start to begin.

I was so glad to get Ryan in Heath's vehicle. We were heading to
Turning Point with no intentions of turning back. I had never been
there but I sure was glad to be there at that time. It was such beautiful country. The large flowing fields were so green with gorgeous
flowers and trees. The scenery grew more beautiful the closer we got
to Turning Point. Ryan looked awful and was in the worst shape of
his life, but thank God we were going to get help for him. I was filled
with hope and knew that God was going to do a great work in Ryan's
life there. The people at Turning Point were fantastic. They were so
warm and kind. We could tell that the Spirit of the Lord was there.
Ryan would feel bad for a few days as he withdrew from the heroin
but would then start one of the best spiritual journeys of his life.
There was a certain amount of time before Ryan could call us, but
I kept in touch with Chris and Jeremy to check on Ryan's progress.
When Ryan was able to call, he sounded like a different person. We
prayed as hard as we ever had for the chains to be broken in his life.
It would be a little time before we could visit him, but we knew he
was in the best place that he could possibly be.

It was probably a blessing to be in the midst of starting a high school soccer program during this time. I did miss a few practice days and it was difficult planning practices and carrying them out, but it did get my mind off of our problems when I was able to focus on the soccer program. We actually got Ryan to Turning Point two days before the start of our first ever soccer season. After running on pure adrenaline during that period of time, I crashed. The second week of soccer season, I missed two days of school, including a game in Mobile, Alabama. In fear of having what I thought was a nervous breakdown, I went back to one of the places that I have felt such peace over the years. I went back to my room at Dad's house and spent a day and a half reading the Bible, talking to God, and talking to each of my three sisters, Elizabeth, Lynn, and Carol. I don't think I left the room except to use the bathroom. God gave me a renewal for life, gave me incredible strength, and brought me out of the deep depression that I thought I was slipping into.

Sunday, March 1, Bethany, my sister Lynn, and I went to Turning Point to visit Ryan for the first time. It was so good to see Ryan. We hadn't seen him in almost a month. He looked really well! He looked so alert and alive. He sounded really mature also. The Lord had been doing a great work in his life those first several weeks. I had great hope that he was going to come through all of this but I continued praying. There had been glimpses of Ryan surrendering his all to God in the past year and a half. I knew that I had seen a miraculous transformation when he first confessed his sins to God, put his trust in Him, and asked Him to come into his life back in August 2013. I know the growth that was taking place in his life before letting his guard down and becoming entrapped by heroin. I held so tightly to the hope that he would give his all to the Lord on a daily basis and move forward in his walk with Jesus. I was cautiously optimistic. I didn't want to experience that horrific, hollow dead feeling in the pit of my soul again. I would have rather died than to go through it again. Would there be joy in our lives again? Would Ryan begin anew with Jesus on the throne of his life? These questions and others like them were to be left up to Ryan and his willingness to allow God to transform him and grow him daily. We prayed fervently for those things. That's all we could possibly do. A few weeks later, I was able to drive up to Bessemer where the guys from Turning Point were going to be taken to church. Wow, was I nervous! I couldn't wait to see Ryan again, hoping that he would look like he did two weeks prior. On the way, I asked God to send a dove as a sign for hope. Seconds later, four doves flew overhead from right to left and across the highway. "Oh, thank you, Lord!" I said.

As I arrived at the church, I saw the Turning Point van in the parking lot. I parked my truck and walked over. Ryan and I spoke briefly before we all went inside the church for the worship service. He looked so sharp with his suit on. The worship service began. At the part where we were greeting everyone, Brother Allen, the pastor, told us to turn to the person beside us and tell them what God has done for you. Ryan turned toward me, hugged me, and said, "He set me free!" I was speechless! I will never forget that moment as long as I live. My whole being was filled with joy, hope, and gratefulness. *Could it be?* I thought to myself. *Could Ryan have surrendered his life totally to God? Let it be, Jesus, let it be.* I thought over and over.

The worship time was amazing! Brother Allen brought a message dealing with the passive mind. The scripture verses were from Romans chapter 12 where the writer, Paul, encourages us not to be conformed to this world but to be transformed by the renewing of our minds. That's exactly what Ryan had been doing at Turning Point, renewing his mind daily by reading the Bible and growing in grace and knowledge of Jesus.

Date: 4-5-15

What an incredible + amazing week! Bethany and I got to visit Southern Miss twice, go to church at Milly Bapt w/ Sandra + Gary, work in the yard, rest, spend time w/ Rebekah, help Brianna + Heath move into their new house and spend time w/ Ryan at Turning Point today. Today was a fantastic end to the Spring Break Week as we witnessed Ryan's baptism in the pond at Turning Point!!!! So did Wayne's family, Nana + Pop got to be there as well. Jesus, You are doing amazing things in Rebekah + Ryan's lives. Continue to lead them + show them how they can use their lives to obediently reach others with The Gospel of Jesus Christ! Lead Ryan + Rebekah to resist the devil + follow You with all of their hearts, souls, minds! Lead us all to separate ourselves from the world + fall deeply in love with You Jesus!

Prepare us to accomplish all that You want us to so You'll receive glory + honor. Give us Power through The Holy Spirit to boldly go + speak Jesus to others Lord —

Amen!!!!

Ryan was growing in the Lord at Turning Point. He was studying his Bible, journaling what God was doing in his life, and speaking at chapel on occasion. I got a small glimpse of what it looked like for him to be a godly leader. Jeremy, who worked at Turning Point, kept me informed about Ryan's progress. The whole time Ryan was at TP,

Bethany and I prayed for not only Ryan, but for revival to break out in all of the hearts of the guys there. It was happening. For the first time in Ryan's life, he was experiencing being around godly guys who wanted to worship and know God more. They were becoming a band of brothers, loving God and loving each other. Ryan told me that he and several others wanted to be baptized there in the pond at Turning Point. It would take place after church on Easter Sunday, April 5, 2015. What a dream come true. We couldn't wait! Bethany and I, Bethany's parents (Nana and Pop), and Bethany's brother's family (Wayne, Leigh, and their children) went to Turning Point for the joyous occasion. Pop hadn't seen Ryan since February. I'll never forget the look on his face when he saw Ryan. He teared up and was about to cry. Ryan looked great. He was beaming with joy. He had gained some weight he had lost and really looked healthy. After we ate lunch, we all headed toward the pond for the main event. We were so excited! Thankfulness filled our hearts for the leaders at Turning Point and for all they were doing to help Ryan and the other guys. We really felt like God took this day from the portals of heaven and gave to us to experience and remind us that there could be joy again if Ryan chose God's way. The feeling that we had at the edge of the pond was quite an overwhelming one. Five guys, including Ryan, were baptized that day. As Ryan walked down into the pond toward Pastor Dave, a flood of emotions ran through my mind and body. Ryan acknowledged Jesus as his Savior and was baptized. He came up out of that water with arms upward, fists clinched as a sign of victory. I wouldn't give up anything for that moment! We spent the rest of the day talking to Ryan, most of the other guys, and the Turning Point staff. It was like a huge family reunion. Such an amazing day! We thanked God for bringing Ryan to this point in his life, through all of the turmoil, pain, and discouragement.

Ryan was able to come home for the weekend of April 10 to 12 for Brianna and Heath's wedding. The wedding was beautiful, and we all had a great time. It was good to see Ryan interacting with family again, smiling, and having a good time. Before taking Ryan back to Turning Point, we met up with Connie, a special friend who loved Ryan and prayed for him consistently for quite some time. Connie and Ryan got to talk a little bit before we had to leave. Several weeks later on May 3, 2016, I went up to Bessemer, Alabama, go to church at Oasis of Praise with the guys from Turning Point. I decided to sit in the balcony and worship quietly by myself, meet Ryan and the guys from Turning Point after church, and follow them back to Thorsby. God poured out His Spirit on me that morning. I, coming from a sometimes legalistic, stiff Southern Baptist background, raised my hands and my voice to God like never before. I praised, knelt in prayer, and was overcome by God's love, mercy, and grace. It was one of most freeing times of worship that I have ever felt in a corporate worship setting. God did a great work in me that day as Brother Mike led in awesome worship and Brother Allen preached the best sermon I've ever heard in my life. Yes, it was on grace. I was beginning to understand just what biblical grace really meant.

Ryan decided to stay an extra week at Turning Point to attend a Men's LIFE conference at the Church of the Highlands in Birmingham, Alabama. LIFE stands for Living in Freedom Every day. Jon and Timothy had been leading a group in the LIFE study at Turning Point. Ryan shared with me that at the conference, he went down the front and a person who prayed with him told him that he was anointed by God to do great things. This was the second time someone who didn't even know Ryan told him that. I had always felt that if Ryan were to ever submit to God's will and way, He would do absolutely unbelievable things through Ryan to reach thousands of people with the Gospel.

10

Miracle Job

Jehovahjireh, the Lord will provide.

Ryan graduated from Turning Point. I picked him up on May 10, 2015. I was so grateful to the entire Turning Point staff for all that they did to encourage, teach, counsel with, and be a friend to Ryan. Even though we were all nervous about Ryan coming home, we hoped that life would be better. Things were going well in the weeks that followed. Ryan was growing in the Lord and our family life was better than it had been in years. Our war zone had been replaced with a peaceful, more joyful place. Rebekah was starting forgive Ryan for those years of embarrassment and pain that he caused. We constantly prayed for Ryan and Rebekah's relationship. They were so close growing up, but this addiction had really destroyed their relationship. Many times people don't think about the siblings of someone who is addicted and how they are affected emotionally. Actually, an addiction has giant ripple effects that reach family members, relatives, and friends. Rebekah seemed to shut down in a sense. She became anxious and quiet. She loved her brother, but the years of lies, embarrassment, and disappointment had turned into resentment. I think it was just easier for Rebekah to not talk about it, not have expectations, and not cultivate more of a relationship with her brother. That is completely understandable. There were times that I talked with Rebekah about our family issues but I hate to say that I closed myself off during difficult times more times than not. That is something that I deeply regret. As bad as things were at times, I still knew deep in my heart that one day Ryan and Rebekah's relationship would be whole again. Bethany and I were hoping that they could reconnect on our family vacation soon.

Several weeks after Ryan came home from Turning Point, we made a trip to Disney World. We had the trip of a lifetime. My dad and stepmom went as well as my family and my two married sisters' families. It turned out to be one of the best vacations that we ever experienced. The memories that we made at Disney World together are some that we will never forget. It was like the early years of our family with laughter, joy, and happiness. Oh, how I want to go back to that place! Things were so alive, fresh, and new. There's just something about being at Disney World that makes you feel like a kid again. Things were continuing to go well for Ryan and our family. He was progressing and getting clean time behind him. He determined in his mind that the girl he spent so much time with doing drugs wasn't good for him, and he wasn't good for her. We were so relieved to hear him say that but continued to pray that he would stay strong.

In early September, Bethany and I needed to have our phones updated. As we were heading down south to Mobile, we noticed an AT&T store that we hadn't seen before. We thought we'd stop by and see if we could save some time by going to that store. As we were getting our phones updated, we started talking with the store clerk. We mentioned that our daughter had graduated from University of Alabama and was looking for a graduate school to attend. The store clerk then said, "You don't have another child living at home who's not in school and looking for a job, do you?"

Bethany and I turned and looked at each other, stunned. "As a matter of fact, yes, we do," I said. One thing led to another, over the next couple of weeks, Ryan filled out an application, had two interviews, and got a job. We were in awe of how the Lord worked that whole thing out. It was no coincidence that it all worked out like that. It was God's providential hand guiding us. Ryan worked there about seven to eight months and did a very good job. He quickly became a favorite of customers going to the store. He also immediately impressed the CEO and other leaders or managers that worked in the company with his work ethic and how he treated customers. During that time, Ryan met a girl who was working for his uncle, in Birmingham, Alabama. They hit it off and eventually dated about 6 months. Ryan settled down and had one of the best runs of sobriety since 2013. I was so thankful for this job and their relationship. We had the best Christmas in recent years. We praised God daily for all of the blessings that He was giving us. We looked forward to 2016 as a year of growth and restoration.

1-1-16
Date: 7:46am

We made it to the year 2016. There were times in early 2015 that I just didn't if we would make it or not. I begged + pleaded to God to help us. He came through with miracle after miracle. 2015 was a year of redemption. The start of something very special in our lives. I believe that the year 2016 will be a year of growth; spiritual, emotional, mental, physical growth. The year 2016 will be a year of growth + restoration; in that order. As we grow by spending time alone with God in Bible reading, fasting + prayer, He will restore "the years the locusts have eaten", Joel 2:25. The year of 2016 will see for the Wright family restoration as individuals before God, restoration with each family member by forgiveness, restoration of our purpose through growth + forgiveness. Restore our minds Lord! Restore our hearts Lord! Restore our bodies Lord! Restore our souls Lord! (Psalm 23:3) Protect us from the evil one + from evil. Give us Godly relationships for encouragement + encouraging. Give us wisdom daily + let us never neglect our time with You God. Lead us to fear You + keep Your commands, and be so joyful in doing so. Let us never forget where we have come from and show us daily where we are going. Lead, guide, direct + give us Godly wisdom + discernment. To God be the Glory !!!

The relationship that Ryan and this girl had was good but at times on again, off again. Ryan really liked her. Bethany and I did too. But she was very wishy-washy, wanting to commit at times and at other times not. This drove Ryan crazy, as it did me. I reminded Bethany that we could definitely deal with ordinary life stuff that most people go through. It was the "out of the ordinary" life things that we had dealt with for several years that were so difficult to handle. The roller-coaster ride that characterized Ryan and this girl's relationship ended not long before Ryan got a job in Birmingham, Alabama. Ryan sought that job in Birmingham at another phone company around April 2016. He filled out the application then was interviewed online and in person. He was hired! We came to find out that most applicants didn't even get an interview, much less get the job that quickly. Another huge blessing from God. He would be making a lot more money but it would entail moving back to Birmingham. It frightened us for him to go back especially since he and this nice girl, which he had been dating for six months, had just broken up. I know that he was feeling rejection from this. *He had made such progress in the last eight months*, we thought. He was taking his medicine the right way, going to church regularly, and moving forward in his life. We went to Birmingham and found him a nice apartment in a gated community. I guess we thought he would be safer in a gated apartment complex. We know now that a gated apartment complex doesn't mean a whole lot if you're not totally committed to staying clean and careful who you let in. I urged Ryan to have absolutely zero tolerance for anyone or anything that would keep him from staying clean. I knew that if the enemy gained even just a little foothold as a result of Ryan letting his guard down, the results could be devastating.

Let me stop here and say that as parents of someone who's fighting addiction, a lot of things go through your minds, and there are many questions that you ask yourself. What did I do wrong? How could I have let this happen? I must be a terrible parent. If I'm a terrible parent, then I'm a failure. The enemy is very cunning. He is very smart. He is very deceptive. He will lie to you over and over to get you down and keep you down. The enemy hates your guts and wants to destroy you, your life, and your family in any way that he can or through anyone that he can. We can't believe the lies that sometimes come to our minds. When we doubt, there are some things we must remember:

1) God will never leave you. You can cast your cares on the Lord. The Bible says that we weren't meant to carry burdens in this life. If you have faith that God will take care of you, then you can give your cares to Him and not worry about the outcome. He will also guide and direct you in the way in which you should go. He knows the past, present, and future. Why not trust in an all-knowing God with your life?

2) God will never fail you. Though bad times may come, though you experience heartache, though at times your life may seem to be falling apart, He will never leave your side, especially in those times that you can reach out to Him. He will hear, He will comfort, and He will give strength. It always helps me to reflect back on my life's most difficult times and remember that God never left me alone. He performed miracles held tightly to my hand and consoled me as I went through those difficulties. That fact helps tremendously when doubt and anxiety begin to flood my mind. Looking back at past miracles and deliverances and looking forward to His promises makes all of the difference.

Also understand that sometimes the enemy will try to torture you through unanswered questions, a certain amount of time you haven't heard from your loved one or just through a rush of anxiousness or fear sent your way for no apparent reason. There are certainly times that God spoke to my heart, telling me that something was definitely wrong. Other times the enemy would send fear and doubt when there wasn't anything going on. The enemy loves to play smoke-and-mirror games to cause us a great deal of stress, unrest, and inner pain. He also does this in hopes that we will not wait upon God and make things even worse by acting too hastily. Remember, there's a war going on. Don't be passive. In those times, these are things you can do to fight:

1) *Read the Bible.* Within the pages of the Bible lie the answers to all of life's issues. It is a serious weapon that must be used in battle. It not only brings comfort in the midst of pain, but it will give you strength and courage in those times of intense spiritual fighting. Saying scriptures aloud and taping scriptures on walls and doors in our house often provided strength that we didn't have. The Bible says in 2 Corinthians 10:3–5 (NKJV), "For though we walk in the flesh, we do not wage war according to the flesh. For the weapons of our warfare *are* not carnal but mighty in God for pulling down strongholds, casting down arguments and every high thing that exalts itself against the knowledge of God, bringing every thought into captivity to the obedience of Christ."

2) *Pray.* Take everything to God—the good, the bad, and the ugly. He wants you to talk with Him about what's going on in your life. He knows already, but there's just something strengthening about talking with and listening to Him as a friend. He wants you to give your burdens to Him.

He is more than able to handle anything. There are times when there is absolutely nothing that you can do about a situation but pray. Thank God we can come to Him in times of need to help us, and He will.

3) *Praise.* Listening to godly music and singing praises to God will uplift your soul. There is power in focusing your mind and thoughts on praises to God to silence the lies of the enemy. God comforts, strengthens, and speaks through godly music. It seems stations such as K-Love always play the right songs at just the right time. Many times the right song gave me enough strength to keep pressing on.

4) *Word of your testimony.* Hearing that there are others who have gone through and are currently going through what you're experiencing helps tremendously. It shows you that you are not alone. By the same token, reaching out to others who are hurting and going through what you have already experienced brings comfort to not only them, but to you also. "And they overcame him by the blood of the Lamb and by the word of their testimony, and they did not love their lives to the death" (Rev. 12:11, NKJV).

5) *The name of Jesus.* There is power in the name of Jesus. The enemy cannot match the power of Jesus. Saying "Jesus" will shake the very gates of hell, cause doors to open, give peace in the midst of the storm, and make demons flee. Say His name boldly. His power transcends all comprehension and can crush the enemy's plans.

6) *Fasting.* When you're trying to clearly hear from God through prayer, fasting is a supernatural way to hear from Him while giving up something (food, electronics, recreation, etc.) so you can instead devote that time to drawing close to and listening to Him. I can't explain it, but I know for a fact that it is effective. "*Is* this not the fast that I have chosen: To loose the bonds of wickedness, To undo the heavy burdens, To let the oppressed go free, And that you break every yoke?" (Isa. 58:6 NKJV).

The enemy will not play fair. He is a liar and a deceiver. Don't play fair with him. After telling us that God resists the proud, but gives grace to the humble, 1 Peter 5:6-11 goes on to say:

Therefore humble yourselves under the mighty hand of God, that He may exalt you in due time, casting all your care upon Him, for He cares for you. Be sober, be vigilant; because your adversary the devil walks about like a roaring lion seeking whom he may devour. Resist him, steadfast in the faith, knowing that the same sufferings are experienced by your brotherhood in the world. But may the God of all grace, who called us to eternal glory by Christ Jesus, after you have suffered for a little while, perfect, establish, strengthen, and settle you. To Him be the glory and the dominion forever and ever Amen. (1 Pet. 5:6–11, NKJV)

Fight the enemy with these supernatural weapons that ensure victory. Fight with boldness and do not give up.

11

***

Not Another Setback

I would have lost heart, unless I had believed that I would
see the goodness of the Lord in the land of the living.
Wait on the Lord; Be of good courage, And He shall
strengthen your heart; Wait, I say, on the Lord!
—Psalm 27:13–14 (NKJV)

Not long after Ryan moved back to Birmingham, he started using heroin again. *Will he ever be able to go back to Birmingham and stay clean?* I thought. It was actually an isolated incident at the time, but about three weeks later, his arm began to get very red and started to swell. It scared the crap out of him, as it should have. He went to the hospital and was admitted. He had an infection in the bend of his arm. It was bad! Twice the surgeon had to cut his arm in two places and squeeze what seemed like a river of pus out of his arm. I was there the second time they did it. It was the worst look of fear I had ever seen on Ryan's face. He knew how horribly bad it would hurt from the first time they drained it days earlier. And hurt it did! He was in excruciating pain. The thing that kept going through my mind was first for me to remain calm so it would help keep him calm. The second thing that went through my mind was the fact that pain can be a good teacher and a good deterrent.

Ryan got out of the hospital and returned to work that next week. He did amazingly well, making good money for several months. In October, He was fighting the urges and cravings of heroin again. I don't know why he didn't call me or his mother. I don't know why he didn't reach out to someone for help. During this time, he wasn't going to any Narcotics Anonymous or Alcoholics Anonymous meetings and wasn't hanging around godly people. He started going to bars with coworkers after work. He went to Church of the Highlands at times but have did to work some Sundays. He had let his guard down and had given the enemy a foothold. It would prove to be devastating. He gave into the cravings in late October. There were again warning signs like long texts that didn't make a lot of sense, other times of silence after we would text him at night, and just the sick feeling in the pit of our stomachs that something could be wrong. Whenever Bethany got those feelings, she was usually right. By the end of November, he was fully addicted to heroin again, probably worse than ever. All of this time he was working forty hours a week making good commission. It just didn't make sense.

Because of the warning signs, I asked Ryan one evening if he was using again. He finally admitted that he was. I asked him if it was bad enough that he needed to go back to Troy for detox and he confirmed. *Oh Lord*, I thought. *Here we go again.* I encouraged him to call and tell his mother so Ryan called and told Bethany what had been going on. Okay, back to survival mode again. We prayed about what to do next. Detox was a must, but where should we go? Ryan had been to The Journey in Troy in early 2015 and they had treated him so well. We decided that The Journey was the place that he should go. I called Don, the manager at The Journey. Good, there was space available. Bethany and I drove three hours north to Birmingham. Of course, God sent doves for us to see along the way to give us hope. Ryan said that he would try to work that day, and we could leave after work at 8:00 p.m. He texted me about fifteen minutes after he got to work saying that he couldn't work that day because he was detoxing and felt horrible. He was so afraid of losing his job. Bethany and I were beside ourselves. Ryan was actively doing drugs again. The thought of him losing this job and all that surrounds this horrible addiction bore down like a ton of bricks. Just before he got back to his apartment from work, he threw up all in his car. He was disgusted with himself. Ryan texted and said that there was no way that he could detox on his own at the apartment. He needed to go to The Journey in Troy, Alabama. He told me that he wanted out of this addiction. He said that he would quit his job and move to the other end of the world if it meant getting clean. He apologized over and over, saying how he hated this addiction. My heart broke with every text but I had to remain calm and encouraging. "This can be overcome through the power of Jesus," I texted back. It was another desperate situation, but I did believe that Jesus was going to rescue him. I believed it with all of my heart. One thing that always helped me to keep fighting and moving forward was to remember the miracles of the past that God had done to save and keep Ryan alive. I would think back to seemingly impossible situations and remember how God moved in miraculous and powerful ways. Also, many, many times God would send doves for me, Bethany, and Ryan to see. Doves had become a sign of God's hope to us. He sent doves often and just at the right time when we were feeling defeated. Our hope, faith, and peace were renewed. We were still very broken people, but these signs from God gave us the strength and courage to continue to press on.

Date: 11-25-16 3:43pm

I love being in the woods Lord! It is so beautiful out here. The sound of squirrels, green + brown leaves all around, the beauty of Your Creation in the gentle breeze, the chirping of the hundreds of crickets before sundown. This is such a pleasant place to be, especially when feeling of distress, despair + disappoint rage inside of me. Thank You Jesus for bringing a calming upon my weary soul, a "peace be still" upon my ears + a gentle touching of my heart knowing that it's going to be OK. Wholeness of children + family are within reach. Bring it quickly Lord on this side of Heaven + on this earth... Redemption surely draweth nigh...

We departed from Birmingham and took him to The Journey on December 3, 2016 and left him there to detox. Those goodbyes are always so gut-wrenching. He should've been there seven days like he was back in early 2015, but for some reason, the insurance would only pay for him staying five days. When I picked him up, I couldn't believe how bad he looked. My first thought was, *He's not ready to be out.* Ryan was very shaky walking out to the car. As we got in the car, he grasped my head on both sides with his hands and said through bitter tears, "Dad, I am so sorry!" He kept shaking his head. "I cannot believe I messed up again!" My heart broke. I tried to tell him that his family would be there for him and see him through this.

As we drove to Birmingham, he expressed wanting to tell his bosses at work what had been going on for over a month. I said that it would be a good idea so he got cleaned up and drove to talk to them. He talked with his bosses for quite some time. They were so understanding and so kind. We appreciated that so much. I can't thank David, Justin, and Jason enough for their kindness, love for Ryan, and willingness to help him. In the days that followed, they would text to ask how Ryan was doing and if there was anything they could do to help. They assured me that they were praying for him.

Sometime before or after the meeting with his bosses, Ryan found more heroin. I guess that the pull of the heroin was so great in his weakened state that he wanted to do a little more before going off to rehab. He agreed with me that a long-term rehab stay would be best. His bosses gave their word that if he was sober for a while, they would give Ryan his job back. The promise of having his job again was such a pivotal aspect for Ryan mentally going to rehab. He was worried about his job and didn't want to lose it. Even though we were facing a year of rehabilitation, we were optimistic because his bosses were so kind and especially because the Holy Spirit was giving us peace in the midst of another storm. The next few days were horrific as I desperately tried to get Ryan to go to a yearlong rehab facility in central Alabama. Ryan did not get readily prepared to go to rehab so I knew that he must still have heroin. It had such a hold on him that he couldn't leave until it was all used or gone. Doesn't make sense but when you're dealing with this type of thing, nothing makes sense. It just ripped my heart out being in that situation. After several days of horror, I finally got Ryan to that yearlong rehab facility. The date was Sunday, December 11, 2016. I got him there at 9:30 a.m. I felt a certain uneasiness leaving him there. I saw fear in his eyes as I told him that everything was going to be okay. I hurt deep within my soul but I did believe that he was going to be okay.

As I drove away, I bellowed and cried so loudly that I could've been heard from miles away. I thought this was going to be the beginning of healing for my son. That facility is a great place that many men have come to know Jesus and beaten addiction, but it turned out to not be the place for Ryan. Trying to see through my tears, I headed home. I passed a big brick church and wondered if I should ask someone to pray for Ryan and our family. I felt the urge to turn around and drive back. I drove into the church parking lot to see three senior citizens standing in the parking lot. I stopped and asked if they could direct me to a deacon or to the pastor so I could ask them to pray for me. One of the gentlemen told me that he was a deacon. His name was Mr. Steen. He was so kind to me. He took me into the church and gathered together three other men. We went to a room where I told them a little of my story. They prayed for Ryan and my family. It was so comforting to know that these people cared enough to pray for someone that they had never met. Mr. Steen invited me to stay for the worship service. I didn't want to stay but I'm so glad that I did. It was a warm, Spirit-filled church that welcomed me with open arms. During the service, Mr. Steen leaned over to me and said that people like me held a special place in his heart because of what he had gone through years ago in his own family. I was thankful that God led me directly to the right person to talk to. That was definitely another divine appointment. Mr. Steen, the pastor, and the church office even continued sending texts and calling in the following weeks saying that they were praying for Ryan and my family. That is what a church is designed to do: equip the believers, reach out to all people with the gospel, and encourage the downtrodden. Thank you, Canaan Baptist Church, for being Jesus to me in a very dark time in my life. I prayed that God would bless that church. I knew that I'd return to thank them one day and share my story of the wonderful grace of God.

God showed me something profound on my way back home. I looked, as Bethany and I always did, to see if I could see a dove flying as I was driving back. I didn't see any. I was a little disappointed and hoped that this wasn't an indication that things would not end well. As I peered out of the truck windows, I felt God speak to me. He told me that even though I hadn't seen a dove, it didn't mean that they weren't there. I looked out at the large green fields on both sides of the road as I was driving and knew that there were doves in the ground in those fields even though I couldn't see them from where I was. It then dawned on me that even though I couldn't see hope, it was definitely there. Even though I couldn't see God, He was definitely there. He was telling me that I didn't need to depend on a dove as a sign that things were going to be okay. I needed to depend solely on Him, the One who sent the doves as signs.

I made it back home and tried to get some sleep but it was difficult. I couldn't begin to count the number of times over the last several years that I would get up in the middle of the night, sit on the couch, pray for my family, or just watch TV because I couldn't sleep. Daystar had a program that came on about 3:00 a.m. each day called *Reflections*. It showed beautiful scenery from around the world as different Bible verses would slowly appear and disappear on the screen. This program brought great healing to my soul. I watched it almost every early morning! I coached varsity sports during the most traumatic of our family difficulties. I was almost used to having a little trouble sleeping because of the coaching, especially after games. I was the head volleyball coach from 2011 to 2016, the head softball coach from 2011 to 2014, and the head soccer coach from 2015 to 2017. I don't think any of my players or even my students at school realized how important they were in my life. I know that my players and students helped me tremendously in dealing with our tragic circumstances. Those players breathed life into me each day. At times, I definitely needed it. I wanted to isolate myself but couldn't because of coaching. I'm very thankful for that. You know, God has a way of sending the right people when we are at our lowest. The encouragement and peace that He gives does *transcend all understanding*. However, the encouragement of loving people is needed just as badly. Those players, students, and supportive parents will never know just how much they meant to me and will always hold a special place in my heart.

12

No Christmas This Year

*Don't get ahead of God. Don't interfere with what
He has planned. Allow God to work.*
—Corporal Benny Paul Washington

The next few days would begin a chain of events that would become some of the most gut-wrenching times that we would endure up to that point. One of the directors at the yearlong facility called me while I was at school the next morning, saying that Ryan wanted to leave. I was devastated. He put Ryan on the phone. Ryan told me that he wasn't fully detoxed and that he had to leave. He said that he had already called someone to come pick him up. I begged Ryan to reconsider or at least stay until I could get someone we trust to come pick him up. I learned from past experiences that in the midst of chaos and uncertainty, I must be calm so I can hear from God. It wasn't easy because I could feel the panic inside my mind and body. I asked God what in the world I should do. I wondered if my sister Lynn was at her home in Vestavia Hills, Alabama. I called her. She answered and said that she could get Ryan and take him to a hospital to detox. Fervently, I prayed God would somehow prevent Ryan from being picked up by whoever he called. If Ryan was picked up before Lynn got there, I wasn't sure if we would hear from him again. I quickly phoned an intake guy from the facility to see if they would take Ryan back after detoxing. The guy said that they would let Ryan come back. Thank God we at least had an option after detoxing. I hung up my cell phone and realized that my first class of the day would soon be starting. As my class entered the gym, I yelled for one of my students to go get the principal. I talked to my principal a few weeks earlier, explaining our issue and asking him to pray for Ryan and our family. Mr. Alford told me to take care of anything that I needed to take care of, he would watch my class. I was so thankful that God had placed another understanding and compassionate person in my life.

Over the next several hours, Lynn took Ryan to several hospitals, but they didn't have detox units. All the while, Ryan's body was starting withdrawal. Lynn drove frantically around Birmingham, trying to find a place for Ryan to detox as he was in so much pain. I was outside of the gym near the baseball field, trying to call different places most of the morning. Jared, a guy I previously talked to about a long-term rehab facility in Eastern Alabama, called and said that he could refer Ryan to Bradford Health Services. He convinced the people at Bradford Health that Ryan needed help right away. Lynn drove Ryan up to Bradford Health. As he was waiting to be checked in, he started throwing up and having a seizure. Immediately, Ryan was taken by ambulance to a nearby hospital emergency room. They put an IV in his arm but didn't hook it up to a bag to give him fluids. As Ryan sat there for almost two hours, Lynn tried to go sit with him in ER. The nurse wouldn't let her go back. To this day, we still don't know why. They told Lynn that they were busy that night, and that's what was taking so long to care for Ryan. I still believe that they thought this was another drug addict so what was the hurry. As the time neared three hours that Ryan was in ER hooked up to nothing, he finally just walked out. No one stopped him. They only gave him a token. "Don't go. It's not in your best interest," which cleared them of liability as they watched him walk right out. Lynn had to leave the hospital about ten minutes prior to Ryan leaving even though she didn't know that he had left. She was going to have to get up at 3:30 a.m. that next morning to catch a five thirty flight. I decided to call to check on Ryan to see how he was doing. The nurse nonchalantly said, "Oh, he left about twenty minutes ago".

I was beside myself. "How could you just let him leave?" I screamed.

She acted very unmoved and unconcerned. I called Lynn to tell her that Ryan had left the hospital. She was so upset. She drove back to the hospital and then around the surrounding areas. She was crying, desperately trying to find her nephew. During this time, I talked to Jared on the phone. He tried finding out from the detox facility's end what had happened. He was so kind during this ordeal and vowed that he would pray for Ryan's return. After looking for a while, I called Lynn, thanked her for looking, and told her that she needed to go home. I know that she felt terrible.

It was about 7:30 p.m. at this time. My son was on the streets of Birmingham, Alabama, with no money, phone, or place to sleep. Words cannot express just how devastated I was. My only hope was that Ryan would find some heroin that somehow wouldn't kill him so he could sleep through the night and call me in the morning. Silently, I felt horrible for hoping such a thing. If you've ever been in a situation like that, you know what I'm talking about. I could not believe this was happening. Why was God putting us through this? Ryan had a place to detox and then the yearlong facility told us that they would take him back. The opportunity was so close and within reach. Why, Lord, why?

Bethany and I prayed for angels to protect Ryan through the night. We decided that Bethany would go to school while I go look-ing for Ryan the next day. Bethany called my oldest sister, Elizabeth, and asked her to pray for Ryan. In the course of their conversation, Elizabeth asked to come with me to look for him. As I waited for Elizabeth to get there, I decided that we would go to Birmingham that night. It was about 11:00 p.m. I wanted to be able to leave early the next morning looking for Ryan. If we went to Birmingham that night, we would be three hours closer. Elizabeth arrived at our house, and we packed the truck and headed for Birmingham. I was so scared. I was so broken. *Lord, surely, this is not how this story is going to end.* The songs that played on the radio from the K-Love station comforted my broken heart and weary soul. Elizabeth and I arrived at Ryan's apartment around 2:00 a.m. She prayed fervently for Ryan using the couch for an altar. Not long after praying, I went to sleep. I was exhausted.

I slept for several hours and woke up a little before 5:00 a.m. "I'm going to look now. There's no time to waste," I said to myself. I got up, splashed some water on my face, and headed out to the streets of Birmingham to search for a needle in a haystack. I was prepared to fight, if need be to find Ryan and bring him to safety. I drove feverishly around the hospital where he was the night before, looking down streets, alleyways, and any place that Ryan could possibly be sleeping. I whispered silent prayers as I drove, asking God to protect him and bring him safely to me. I even looked near a few places that I thought were drug hangouts. I decided to go to the hospital emergency room where Ryan had been the night before to get a clue of his whereabouts. I talked to the guy at the information desk. He said that he was there when Ryan left. He wasn't much help and didn't seem to care much either. I didn't know what to do. As I walked outside in disappointment, I noticed a police officer walking to his police car. He was a big man, standing about six foot five. Out of desperation, I stopped him and told him my story. He looked at me with such compassion as I attempted to talk. I cried as I explained the situation and asked what I should do. I was scared to death. My faith waned and my heart groaned within me. I was gripped with fear and anxiety.

Corporal Washington looked me straight in the eye and said, "This is a divine appointment." I was stunned. But the words that Corporal Washington said pierced through the darkness that I was feeling. They calmed my fears, calmed my anxieties, calmed my shaking body, and brought peace and a stillness that only comes from Jesus. He had gone through something similar in his family also. "Ryan is a believer," he said. "God will not leave him nor take His hand off Ryan's life."

"I believe," I quietly replied. And I really did. I knew that either way, it was going to be okay.

Corporal Washington talked to me about his own family and how God miraculously saved them in their own desperate situations. "If God worked this miracle in my son's life, why would you think that He wouldn't do it for your son? Don't get ahead of God. Don't interfere with what He has planned. Allow God to work. Before the foundation of the world, God knew this would happen. It did not surprise Him. He has a plan." Corporal Washington passionately prayed the blood of Jesus to be over Ryan. He prayed for angels to keep Ryan safe. I felt such peace because I knew that those words came directly from God. I hugged Corporal Washington and decided not to get ahead of God. Corporal Washington got Ryan's description and said that he would look for him and pray for him to be found. He gave me his number and told me to let him know if Ryan contacted me.

As I went back to my car, I thought, *I have no earthly idea what You're doing, Lord, but I am going to stick with You and silently wait for Your salvation. I want to beg for mercy for Ryan, dear Savior. See him through this dark time and bring him to rich fulfillment.* I decided that I would check out one more place to look for Ryan. While driving, I got a text from a number I didn't recognize. It was at 7:40 a.m. The text said, "Call me. It's Ryan. I'm using someone's phone." "Thank God!" I shouted. I called Ryan immediately and headed to the place to meet him. There was a wreck on the road so it took me twenty minutes. It seemed like two hours! I called Corporal Washington, told him the great news, and thanked him for being there for me. I picked Ryan up almost two hours after talking with Corporal Washington. The Lord, like so many times before, had placed a godly person in our path to calm me and provide me with encouragement in a very anxious and desperate time.

That evening, Jared called and said he could get Ryan into a hospital in Eastern Alabama for detox then to a yearlong rehab from there. Ryan agreed to go. My sister Elizabeth, Ryan, and I headed for the hospital. It was several hours away, which gave Ryan time to get some sleep. We arrived at the hospital and waited for Ryan to be checked in and orientated. He was supposed to be there five to seven days before going to the rehab facility. Ryan commented that the cost to stay at the rehab was bothering him because that was a lot of money. But money didn't matter at this point. I wanted my son to get treatment no matter the cost. Ryan, Elizabeth, and I actually had a good time in the hospital for the four or five hours that we were there checking him in and getting various tests. We laughed, joked, and told stories. I saw that big beautiful smile that Ryan was known for during that time. I had to remind myself that he was about to detox in that hospital shortly. We just tried to focus on talking and laughing with each other. Then it was time for us to leave. Ryan got quiet. We knew that from the previous weeks that this wasn't a good thing. Elizabeth and I wanted to cry, but we had to go. It's an excruciating thing to leave your child in someone else's hands and drive two or three hours away knowing that they're going to experience intense mental, physical, and emotional pain. We told him, like we always did, to fight this and ask God for help. Again we bid goodbye and prayed for God to work in his life. It was yet another time of stepping out into the scary unknown.

Ryan was at that hospital for detox for only three days, December 13–16. I received a phone call from someone at the hospital telling me that Ryan and two other guys left the hospital. They called a cab to come get them. That sick feeling I had grown accustomed to deep in the pit of my stomach returned. He's back on the streets. I was beginning to wonder if this nightmare would ever end. About an hour later, I saw that I had three missed calls from a Kentucky number. I quickly called but no one answered. I left a voice mail, asking for the caller to call me back. As it turned out, the phone belonged to one of the guys Ryan left the hospital with the night before. I talked with the guy for a while, telling him that I'd be praying for him and that if he heard from Ryan to let me know. Within the hour, I got a text from Ryan from another number at 9:46 a.m. asking me to call him. He was so confused, not really knowing why he left the hospital. I knew it was because of the pull of heroin. There was this intense war that was going on, not a war for his soul, but a war to stop what God had planned for Ryan's life. He told me that if Bethany and I would come get him, he would go back to Bradford Health for detox. From there, he asked to go to Turning Point. What choice did we have? There were no guarantees that the Bradford Health would even take him back because he might be considered a *flight risk*.

I called Jared, and he got in touch with the facility. Amazingly, Jared was able to talk with someone who gave Ryan another chance there. That was pivotal. I was so thankful for not only Jared going beyond the call to help Ryan, but also for the calmness in Jared's voice each time we talked. I was also thankful that the administrator at Bradford Health had compassion for Ryan and sought to help him. During this time, we were reaching out to many people to pray for my son. I texted Mary Louise from House of Hope and asked her to pray for Ryan. The next day, she called and encouraged me in the Lord. She also told me about the two visions she had, one of me and one of Ryan. She saw me fervently praying for Ryan, enclosed in a crystal globe of some sort. As I was praying, demons were trying to get to me to stop praying but God was protecting me. She also saw Ryan enclosed in a crystal prism of some sort. He was safe from the demons trying to get to him because he was covered in the blood of Jesus. This was another confirmation from God that even though we were not sure of what would happen next and we didn't know how everything would play out, God was going to keep Ryan safe and take care of him.

After finding out where Ryan was, I picked him up then we went back to his apartment. We were there the better half of the day. Bethany and I took him to the Bradford Health on Saturday, December 17. He went willingly. We prayed that this would be the last time that he would go through this. Ryan agreed that he needed long-term care but told us that he couldn't go to the yearlong facility because he couldn't bear to have us pay that large fee. He added that there wasn't even a guarantee that he would stay for a year. So Turning Point was the only option this time. Pastor Dave said Ryan could stay much longer than the usual three months. So the plan was for Ryan to go from Bradford Health to Turning Point for a year. Ryan knew and respected Pastor Dave and the leadership at Turning Point. He felt like this was the place he needed to go. We were so tired and weary. At times we thought we were losing battle after battle, even the war was in jeopardy of being lost. Ryan put his body through so much. "Please, God, see us through. Please see us through," we prayed.

The seven days that Ryan was at the Bradford were unnerving. We had just gone through the worst month of our lives, and there were just no guarantees that he was going to stay. I'd go to our city park and just walk around the track for hours talking to God, asking questions, praying, and wondering how this thing was going to end. It was such a somber time. December had been such a roller-coaster ride. I at least was glad to know that Ryan was getting the help that he needed at a care facility. Ryan was there from December 17 to 24. Several times I talked to him, I didn't have a good feeling. Ryan was very quiet, which was not a good sign. He told me that he was trying to figure things out. I talked with two of his counselors. One guy said that Ryan was not ready to give up on heroin. The other counselor said Ryan was participating very little in group sessions and seemed disinterested. A few days later, she did say that Ryan seemed better, smiling more and participating more. That was what I was praying to hear. When the day came for Ryan to leave detox, a friend of ours, Keith, picked him up and took him to his apartment. Ryan had a lot of respect for Keith. But as much as Keith tried to reason with him about going to Turning Point, it didn't work. A phone call from Keith told me that Ryan was not willing to go to Turning Point. It was Christmas Eve. I did the only thing I could do. I said goodbye over the phone and put Ryan in God's hands. That was my only option. I wasn't going to Birmingham to get him and try to talk him into anything. The desire to get clean and stay clean would have to come from Ryan. I had done all that I could do. As I took a somber walk down my street later that day, I looked up to see a dove of hope sitting on the telephone wire. "Thank you for sending that dove, Lord. Even though I don't know how this is going to end and even though I am completely broken, I will continue to hope in You."

Christmas day came and went, but I didn't participate with my family. It was just too painful. Christmas had always been such a joyous time of the year for our family. My mother made sure of that. Bethany and I always saw to it that our children had a good Christmas each year as well. We believed those Christmas traditions were so important to have. But the thought of not having Christmas really didn't even enter my mind. I was too heartbroken to even care, I guess. I really don't remember much of what I did during those days before, during, and after Christmas. Mostly I went to the park and walked around the track for hours and hours, talking to God and trying to reconcile in my mind somehow all that had happened. How could we have gotten to this low point so quickly? Ryan was just doing so well at his new job in Birmingham then a few short months later, we are in utter despair. Those days were such a blur. As bad as things had been at different times before, I knew that this was one of the lowest points of my life.

13

— • —

Is This the End?

God can take your deepest sorrows and turn them into your deepest joys.

Two of Ryan's friends, Tal and Jon, called and texted him often during this time, encouraging him to get help at Turning Point before it was too late. I so appreciated their efforts to help Ryan. They loved him and wanted to see him well as I did. Beth Defranco who worked with Ryan since June was so faithful to call, text, encourage, and pray for Ryan. She was there for our family during some of the darker times in December. Looking back, I know that all of their calls and texts really made a difference. The calls, texts, and prayers set the stage for what was to happen next. After all of those trips traveling to Birmingham, getting Ryan to this, and that detox and rehab, I made a decision that I thought would quite possibly bring all of this to an end one way or another. I still loved Ryan with an everlasting love, but it was time to give him an ultimatum, let him make the decision to get help or not, and allow him to suffer the consequences. He could receive our help or live on the streets. I couldn't do anymore to help, and I was prepared to stand by that decision. That was, by far, the hardest thing that I had to do because it involved relinquishing what I wanted and putting everything on Ryan. I was placing everything in God's hands. There was absolutely nothing more that I could do.

I had been through hell on earth and experienced many horrendous feelings, but that was the worst feeling I have ever experienced.

I texted Ryan as Bethany, Elizabeth, and I drove to Birmingham. I told him that this was it. This would be rock bottom for him, leaving him with nothing. No place to live, no car, no job, and no way to pay for his phone, car, or student loan. His credit would be destroyed. I told him that even though I loved him so very much, I wasn't helping him with those anymore. It hurt me deep within my soul, but it was definitely what I needed to do to keep my sanity. This was killing me and Bethany slowly. The thought of not knowing what would become of him gnawed at my heart. I asked the Lord for strength to withstand whatever happened. I texted to ask him to be at the apartment by three thirty or I would assume that he didn't want any help. I desperately held to the hope that God would bring about a miracle in Ryan's life, but my faith was waning.

This was the following conversation between me and Ryan by text:

- 3:21 p.m., Ryan said, "I said I was coming bc I am I just am trying to get to where I look okay and then I'm heading straight there. And I'm ready to sit until I take my detox meds."
- 3:26 p.m., I said, "I want to cut the time off at 3:30, but Aunt Elizabeth wants me to give just a little more time. Idk. I know that I'm not waiting 'til 6:00. I've got to have a specific time."
- 3:33 p.m., Ryan said, "I would think within the hour. I mean I just want to make sure I'm OK to drive. The positive thing is that I'm coming as soon as possible."
- 3:58 pm., Ryan said, "I'm ready to be there, trust me."(Oh no! I had not thought of whether he was able to drive or not. *I can't press him right now*, I thought. I wouldn't forgive myself if he crashed and was hurt or hurt someone else. I didn't have any choice but to give him more time.)
- 4:31 p.m., Ryan said, "I am getting to the point that I'm where I'm almost alright. I would just be safe than fall

asleep and endanger myself and possibly someone else...
but anyway, I'm leaving in 15 min. on the dot." (There was
hope. "God, please let it be so, let it be so," I cried)
- 4:44 p.m., I replied, "It's been 13 min. since you said you
  were leaving in 15 on the dot."
- 4:50 p.m., Ryan said, "I know. I'm taking my stuff to the
  car now."

I took a chance and called Ryan at 5:03 p.m. We hadn't talked
on the phone in five days. I dialed his number and placed the phone
on the floor where I was kneeling. *Oh my gosh*, he answered! He's
coming! "Ryan! Ryan, where are you?" I exclaimed. He said that his
phone wasn't charged but that he was headed toward the apartment.
About that time, he said that he hit a median. His car wasn't driving
right, and he couldn't explain where he was. I told him to pull off the
side of the road, and we would come get him.

- 5:12 p.m., Ryan said, "My phone is on 14%."

So Bethany, Elizabeth, and I went looking for him. He called
me back at 5:23 and 5:33 p.m. He was so worried and disoriented.
He told us that he was parked near an exit. Between those phone
calls, I called my sister Lynn who lived in Birmingham to ask her
where the exit might be where he was parked. His last call came at
5:37 p.m. when he said that he had a one-percent charge left on his
phone. Soon after, his phone got cut off. We prayed and asked God
to keep him calm and help us find Ryan. As we were driving around,
we saw his hazard lights on. This was at 5:49 p.m. "There he is!"
we all exclaimed. We had to keep going around the interstate and
take the exit that we thought he was in. As we drove up, we saw him
standing beside his car, crying, and looking for us. It was 5:54 p.m.
We ran to him and hugged him, saying, "I love you, I love you!" He
was paranoid, saying that he thought someone was following him.
We walked him over to my truck.

As he got in, he kept asking, "Am I safe? Am I safe?"

"Yes, you are. We've got you, Ryan," we assured him. I would have fought anyone in the world to keep him in that truck. "Thank you, Jesus!" I kept whispering to myself.

We got him something to eat and got him back to the apartment. I called Pastor Dave to see if Ryan could come to Turning Point that night. Pastor Dave said for us to bring him on. While I was on the phone, Ryan was gathering up his clothes. Ryan urged us to hurry and take him to Turning Point. We loaded up and got him there at 7:15 p.m. The people at Turning Point were so kind. They allowed me to stay the night with Ryan in the staff house because he had been through such a traumatic time. When Ryan got settled in on the couch, he asked again, "Am I safe?"

I assured him, "Yes, Ryan, you're safe."

He said, "Dad, my mental state is very fragile right now." He went on to say that for some reason, heroin really had the hooks in him this time. He also alluded to that fact by text a few times in the passing weeks. It scared me for him to tell me that but I assured him that everything was going to be okay. He laid down on the couch and slept all night. I quietly wept and thanked God for Ryan's rescue. We were safe in the staff house at Turning Point. I felt as though the weight of the world had been lifted off of my shoulders. I probably thanked God hundreds of times before I drifted off to sleep. I left Ryan there the next day with expectations of a safe recovery. He was in a good place. He was with good people who loved him and wanted to see him succeed. I was absolutely exhausted yet thankful that he was at Turning Point. Little did I know that this time of safety would be short-lived. In just two weeks, we would face another huge challenge, a challenge that I honestly didn't know how God was going to work out.

It was January 12, 2017. I was in the woods hunting deer in a green field. My phone rang. It was Pastor Dave from Turning Point. I gulped. With the events that had taken place over the last month and a half, phone calls from rehabilitation facilities had not been a good sign at all. I nervously answered the phone. Pastor Dave said that Ryan left the facility. With all that we'd gone through, this phone call was the most devastating. We had been through so much to rescue him time and time again. God kept Ryan alive and provided a way of escape each time. But this time, I had no assurance that it would end well. I said out loud, "I don't know how You're going to work this one out, Lord." I buried my forehead in the dirt outside of the shooting house. I trembled, sobbed, and wept bitterly. My hands shook, as did my head. I felt as though I was losing my mind. I said, "No, God, no!" and "What are we going to do?" over and over again. There's no doubt that the authorities would've gotten a call to come pick me up if they saw me during that time. This was beginning to go beyond pain, disappointment, and distress. "God, You've got to help us," I muttered as I tried to sort things out in my mind. "It can't end like this, Lord. It can't end like this!" I was losing all hope and felt like I was breaking down mentally. Rocking back and forth, the pain was excruciating. I knew that I needed to talk to someone very soon.

I texted my friend, Scott Myers. He had been a dear friend for years. He knew our situation and even counseled with Ryan on many occasions. He texted me back and said that he could talk. I called and talked to him for about ten minutes. I told him that I was losing my mind and didn't want to be here anymore. I had *had* enough heartbreak. That was it. I wanted no more of this hell on earth that was my life. Scott prayed for me and tried to console me, but I was crying uncontrollably and was almost inconsolable. Then he said something that cut through the agony I was feeling. Scott told me that he believed all of the horrific emotions I was experiencing were meant for Ryan, but they were being heaped upon me. I thought back to those times when Ryan had migraine headaches as a child and teenager. I used to ask God to give me his headaches so I could bear his pain. Scott said that he believed that I was experiencing that intense spiritual battle on Ryan's behalf. It made perfect sense. I know that God gave Scott those words to tell me. That surely was a difficult phone call for Scott as well, but God calmed me down through that conversation. The pain was still there but I was beginning to think a little more clearly.

I left the green field and headed for the dirt road where I would meet up with Pop, Bethany's dad. I fell into his arms as I told him what had happened. He kept telling me over and over that things were going to be okay and that we were going to make it through this. Pop is an overcomer and knew a lot about tough times during his early years. He had always been like my second father and loved me like his own son. I was still so broken and weary that I just couldn't call and tell Bethany what had happened. I called my sister Elizabeth and asked her to tell Bethany for me. It hurt me so much knowing that Bethany was about to hear the terrible news about Ryan. Instead of calling, Elizabeth and Gary drove an hour to our house to tell Bethany. Before they arrived, Bethany read a Facebook post from Scott desperately asking people to pray and "flood the gates of heaven on behalf of someone who is being held captive by Satan through the addiction of drugs." He went on to say, "I am asking God to send His angels to war on behalf of this person in order to set this captive free." Over two hundred people were praying for Ryan! When Elizabeth and Gary arrived at our house, the Lord had already told her in her heart what had happened.

I still couldn't figure out why Ryan left Turning Point when things seemed to be going so well. I found out later some of the reasons that made Ryan leave. First, He was on antidepressants that were prescribed to him while at the detox facility. Ryan had never taken antidepressants before. He said that they were making him feel crazy and told me that he just couldn't cope with it. He felt like he was in a cage. Secondly, a guy at Turning Point earned a weekend pass and brought back drugs, and Ryan partook. Obviously, there was a terrible war going on inside Ryan's mind and body. For whatever reason, Ryan didn't turn to God to help him so he left. This hurt his mind-set and allowed the enemy a foothold again. It seemed that each time he went back to the streets and to heroin, he was drifting a little farther away from us. The next day, my brother-in-law Gary offered to drive me to Birmingham to hopefully talk with Ryan and bring him back home. Gary and I traveled to Birmingham in hopes of convincing Ryan to ride home with us. Gary talked with Ryan on the phone and poured out his heart to him. We could feel the war that was raging for Ryan's life. Gary was so kind. He sat patiently for several days and was now pleading with Ryan on the phone. But we went home empty-handed. It was a terrible blow to us, but God allowed me and Gary a lot of great conversation during our ride to and from Birmingham. There was a certain amount of healing inside of me as I shared my feelings and asked hard questions about life. I've never been able to adequately express my deep, inner feelings so it helped me mentally, physically, and emotionally to express them to someone. Gary listened to all I had to say. I was so thankful for his willingness to take the time to not only drive and listen to me pour out my heart, but to also comfort me with words of encouragement.

14

---•---

Headed toward Restoration

Step back and just let God be God.
—Victor Castro

As brokenhearted as Bethany and I were, we began to reconcile the fact that Ryan may not come back. Bethany was much stronger than me to stay away. I told Bethany that we needed to go to my friend's church, Casa de Luz (House of Light) in Elberta, Alabama, and ask my pastor friend Raul Salazar and the church to pray for us. We were not giving up. We just wanted prayer to keep strong no matter the outcome. Raul and the people of Casa de Luz fervently prayed for Ryan for several years. They are an awesome group of believers who are real friends. And, man, do those people pray!

During the most discouraging times, I tried to always pray and plead on Ryan's behalf. To be honest, there were times when I didn't pray. I was weary from the fight. I believed that Jesus was intervening on my behalf with words better than what I could choke out. At times the pain was so great that all I could do was sit in silence. This time when Ryan left Turning Point, it did something to me. I told God that if this didn't work out, it wouldn't be because I didn't fervently pray or have many others fervently pray. We're about to engage in all-out war against the enemy and shake the gates of hell. There was going to be bloodshed and death, and our prayer was that it was going to be the death of this addiction. I decided in mid-December to ask people from all fifty states and even people in different countries to pray for Ryan. I'd stay up late searching the Internet for prayer groups or churches that would lift Ryan up in prayer. I knew that God was the only One in the universe that could save Ryan now. I successfully contacted churches, prayer groups, or organizations in all fifty states and had them pray for Ryan's restoration and deliverance from heroin. Many of them e-mail me back. Several kept contacting me even into March 2017 with prayers. We also had people praying for Ryan in Malaysia, Peru, Canada, and England. We actually had a missionary cousin of mine praying for Ryan from North Pole, Alaska!

Bethany and I went to Casa de Luz on Sunday, January 15, 2017. Raul had us come down to the front of the church so they could lay hands on us and offer up prayers for Ryan and for my entire family. The Spirit of the living God was in that place. We felt hope and comfort as the people prayed for Ryan, me, Bethany, and Rebekah. Even though we didn't know where Ryan was, I had a feeling that everything was going to be okay. It was one of the most uplifting worship services that I have ever been a part of. A member of Casa de Luz, Victor Castro, told me after the worship service, he had a word from God for me. Victor allowed God to speak through him to tell me that God would take care of Ryan. I had to let go and try not to do it on my own. He told me about the story of the prodigal son and of Peter walking on the water. Victor said that if I kept my eyes on the Lord, He would handle it. I just had to back up and leave the fight to God. The Lord gave me and Bethany a renewed hope for Ryan and strengthened us immensely in the process. During that worship service, it was truly amazing to see the transformation from downcast and losing hope to being renewed and revitalized with tremendous peace, faith, and hope for the future.

1-16-17 8:41am

Date:

Just when I thought I've reached a new low in life, something else happens. But when I feel like we're at the bottom, God sends doves to remind us of his Hope + Faith + Peace. When I feel I'll lose my mind, God sends someone who can clarify + comfort me. When I feel crushed, defeated, destroyed, God strengthens, encourages + imparts peace that absolutely well just like He's doing as I'm writing, sending a dove to land on a branch in the tree right beside me to sing + tell (above me) towards All understanding. I thank God for sending people + doves to keep me sane + know that He is working every second to get Ryan to recovery, then to rich fulfillment + purpose.

Whatever You're doing Lord, Whatever You have planned for our future. I know with 100% certainty + beyond a shadow of a doubt, that You're preparing us to reach Hundreds of thousands of people with the Gospel. The only way for us to be fully equipped to accept + finish this challenge, this assignment, this purpose for our being on this planet is for us to undergo the horrific, terrible, gut wrenching, stomach churning, agonizing, circumstances that we're currently going through. Thy will be done. Save my son.

Why was I surprised? We had thousands of people praying for Ryan. God gave us a word from His own lips at Casa de Luz just three days earlier. Why was I surprised what God did next? He had done so many miracles, saved Ryan's life too many times to count, and constantly gave us strength, peace, and hope throughout the last several years in the midst of the most horrifying circumstances.

January 18, 2017 was the day Ryan texted and asked me and my brother-in-law Gary to come get him from where he was in Birmingham. We had a volleyball banquet that night so I told Bethany to please handle the program in my place if I wasn't back. Gary and I arrived at the meeting place and sat in the truck as Ryan and I texted each other. We had to pay a little money that he owed and wait for a few hours, but Ryan was able to leave with us that morning at 9:45. I could never repay Gary for the kindness that he showed in those three trips to Birmingham we made together. He was just another example of someone reaching out to me in a desperate time of need. Between December 3, 2016 and January 18, 2017, I made eight trips from my home to Birmingham, Alabama. Bethany went with me a few times, as did Elizabeth. Gary, my brother-in-law, traveled with me three times. It's a three-hundred-mile, round-trip journey. But I didn't think about the miles or about the time involved. I just wanted to save my son and go wherever I needed to go to get him help and healing.

We brought Ryan home to recover. I didn't know what move was next. Do we go back to Turning Point or another facility in the near future? I had enough of Ryan's withdrawal medicines to get through the week, but withdrawing at home had not worked at all in the past. Obviously we stayed on our faces in prayer, seeking God's guidance and direction. Now I wouldn't at all recommend to anyone detoxing at home without medical supervision. It's dangerous and could lead to seizures, dehydration, or other complications. For us at this time, with enough withdrawal medication, we detoxed at home. Ryan was never alone though. We always had someone there with him. To our utter amazement, Ryan's withdrawal time from heroin was not very bad. As a matter of fact, it was rather mild. I could feel God working in miraculous ways, pushing the darkness that drugs bring out of Ryan's mind and body. Even though I didn't know what was next, we decided to continue to take it a day at a time just as God had told Victor to tell me that we should. We were not to try to figure things out. God would have to lead every step of the way. Adopting that attitude was actually very freeing.

Ryan started contacting his uncle again about investments, business, etc. They had been corresponding back and forth for a year or so until about the last couple of months. Uncle Joe was a highly successful businessman and lived abroad for many years. Uncle Joe sent Ryan book after book about behavioral economics, business, and finance. Ryan read every book that was sent to him. Those books gave Ryan the knowledge, background, and desire to start his own business. Those books also provided enthusiasm and drive to stick with the process. Not only did Ryan read those books, but he also took very meticulous notes in composition books about each book that he read. Little did we know but the more Ryan read, journaled, and took notes, the stronger he became. Ryan told me that he believed that God gave him for his purpose on earth, the desire to help others out of difficult situations and addiction and show them how to take control of their finances as well as realize and fulfill their purpose on earth. God has moved in amazing ways since January 18, 2017. This has been the best year that we've had since 2009. Ryan is asking spiritual questions. God is speaking to Ryan and drawing him back into a strong relationship with Him. Ryan has a renewed fire to establish and run his own business. I'm seeing a determination and mind-set that can help him turn his back on heroin for the rest of his life and never return. My prayer is that Ryan as well as my daughter, Rebekah will progress each day and allow God to take total control of their lives and fulfill all that God has for them.

I used to say that in the midst of Ryan's addiction, our family lost precious years. Well, in a sense, we did. We can't go back and start over. We can't unsay or undo the things we said or did over the years. Our home was a battlefield where many wars were fought. But I read a passage of scripture that assured me that God would make all things right if Ryan—as well as Rebekah, Bethany, and I—would choose to allow God to change us and use us to fulfill what He has for us on this planet. Joel 2:25–27 talks about God promising to "restore the years that the locusts have eaten." An addiction can very well feel like a swarm of locusts coming in your life or the lives of family members. It devours relationships, hopes, dreams, and great amounts of time. It's hard to fight against. But God's Word is true. It can be trusted. God assured me a long time ago that the promises of these verses, by way of the changing of Ryan's heart, will make a way for God to restore the *lost* years, and He will pour out His Spirit upon our family. We will have good times for bad, be given opportunities for missed chances, and bestowed "beauty for ashes" (Isa. 61). I am already starting to see this.

15

---·---

The Best is Yet to Come

Scars are what remind us of God's saving power and healing.

At the time of this writing, we're seeing a lot of growth. Praise God! Ryan has been searching for a solid faith that is his—not mine, his mother's, his granddad's, or his grandmama's—a faith that is his. He is proud of who he is for the first time in his life. He feels good about where his life is headed and about his purpose. He's reading a ton of books about business, finance, investing, and behavioral economics. He's writing his prayers in a daily gratitude journal, we're attending church together, and we're laughing and spending time together. He cares deeply about those people who are less fortunate, looked down on by society, and hurting and struggling. He's expressed how disgusted and even angry he is because these people are forgotten, *thrown away*, and not treated fairly because of the color of their skin, because of a bad decision they've made, or because they've been told that they don't "measure up" by people who think they're better than everyone else.

In our search for truth and meaning in a world full of chaos, the Bible says that our search will lead us to Jesus because He is Truth. In the Bible, Jeremiah 29:11 talks about the plans of a hope and a future that God has for us. If you read on to Jeremiah 29:13–14 (NKJV), it says, "And you will seek Me and find *Me* when you search for Me with all of your heart. I will be found by you, says the Lord, and I will bring you back from your captivity." If Ryan will keep his eyes on God's truth, fight and stay on guard against the enemy, and continue to not care what society thinks or will say about his story, then God will use him and actually our entire family to reach hundreds of thousands of people. Many years, ago the Lord showed me that He would reach that many people with the gospel through our family. I'm beginning to believe that God will reach more. I'm seeing a progression in Ryan, a strong determination and courage to fulfill his purpose on this planet. There is a fight to persevere that is starting to take hold. He is focused on starting a business, seeing it succeed, and helping others in many different ways. Sometimes I wonder why Ryan's life was spared. I'm convinced that it's to share his story of redemption with others. Thank you, Jesus Christ, for never leaving us nor forsaking us. Thank you for saving my son's life time and time again. Thank you for giving us all that we've needed to fight, endure, and conquer. Thank you for giving us the opportunity to share our story so that the world will see that there is hope in Jesus.

Dear reader, you may have made bad decisions, wasted years, and seemingly ruined your life. You may think that you've lost many battles and that the war is virtually over. You may feel unloved, unworthy, and undeserving. There may be many questions that you don't have answers for. Reject the lies that the enemy tells you. Do not let them beat you down and take away your joy. Repent of your sins and put your faith and your trust in Jesus, not the fleeting things of this world. Stand and fight! Will you still have times of pain and struggle? Absolutely! Will there still be times of uncertainty? Yes. But as I have experienced firsthand many, many times, Jesus will come to your rescue. He will comfort, heal, and empower you to fight as you put on the armor of God (Eph. 6:10–13) daily. You have spiritual weapons at your disposal that can help you win in the war for your soul and for your life. Those spiritual weapons of the Word, prayer, and praise will carry you to victory through Jesus Christ. In the midst of your victory, He will empower you to discover and fulfill your purpose on this planet.

You are loved! You are treasured! You have a great purpose on this planet! As long as there is breath in your body, you must believe that you can change your world and the world for other people. There's no better time to start than right now. Get up right now and write down five goals that you have for the future. Ask Him to help you a day at a time to work toward reaching those God-planted goals. Ask God what your purpose is on this planet and ask Him to help you fight every day to make a difference through that purpose. When you hit a wall on your way to your goals—and you will—find another way or go right through it. When you fall down—and you will—get back up immediately. When you experience opposition—and you will—listen to God, not to people. You have but one life. Be determined to make it count in light of eternity. Yes, there's a war going on, but you are a warrior. You will fulfill your purpose. Fight in the power of the Lord. Now is your time! The best is yet to come.

> But we have this treasure in earthen vessels, that the excellence of the power may be of God and not of us. *We* are hard-pressed on every side, yet not crushed; *we are* perplexed, but not in despair; persecuted, but not forsaken; struck down, but not destroyed—always carrying about in the body the dying of the Lord Jesus, that the life of Jesus also may be manifested in our bodies. (2 Cor. 4:7–10, NKJV)

Letters to My Family

To my daughter, Rebekah

My dearest Rebekah, I am so sorry that you've had to go through all of this. Over the years, you've seen your brother act like a fool and make terrible decisions. You've been embarrassed, angry, disappointed, and hurt. This has made you go into a shell and experience anxiety and fear. Just when things would get better and you would let your guard down, he would make more bad decisions. I know that you've tried to distance yourself from your brother at times, even though it hurt you to do so. I am sorry that I neglected you at times because of the disruption in our family.

I tried to raise you and Ryan to love the Lord and fulfill your purpose here on this earth. You are a precious young lady, and I know that you will help so many people who have siblings that are fighting this battle in their own lives. I know that you love Ryan very much and want to see him healed. You and Ryan have shared so many great times together in years gone by. You two will be close again very soon. Your prayer to see Ryan healed will be answered. Forgive him and don't ever stop praying for him.

I want you to know that I am so proud of you. You have worked so hard to earn your bachelor and master's degrees in speech pathology, and I know that you'll reach thousands of people and bring joy to their lives because of your great love and compassion for them. God will use you in ways that you never imagined. I am proud of the young woman that you are becoming. You are amazing! I am so thankful that God made you my daughter. You are beautiful inside and out. As long as there is breath in my body, I will be here for you. I love you dearly, Rebekah.

*****

To my wife, Bethany

You are the love of my life, Bethany. At the time of this writing, we have been married for twenty-seven years plus five years of dating. You do not deserved the pain and agony that you have gone through over the past 8–9 years. I am so sorry that you've had to endure all of this. I am sorry for the times when we fussed and fought because we differed in opinion on how to handle the trouble we've experienced. I am also sorry for the many times when I didn't talk to you, silently went to sleep without telling you good night, and when I ostracized myself from you because of the pain I was feeling. I am also sorry for the many times that I took my pain out on you. I am just so happy that there are great days ahead. God has promised to repay the years that the locusts have eaten away. I believe this to be true. We will have many joyful days ahead of us, praise God.

I am so proud of you, Bethany. You are the best person I know. You have loved our children unconditionally, prayed for them and for us consistently, and loved God fervently. You are the definition of what the Bible says that a godly woman is. He blessed me more than words could ever say by putting you in my life. I never would have made it through twenty-seven years of teaching school, twenty-eight years of coaching varsity sports, ten years of youth ministry, and life's ups and downs without your love and encouragement. I know that you have reached thousands of students during your twenty-plus years of teaching, and you will reach thousands more in the future as you share God's mercy and grace through our past troubles. You are amazing!

Let's grow old together, fulfilling God's purpose for our lives. I am proud of the woman that you are. As long as there is breath in my body, I will be here for you. Bethany, you are my hero, and I love you more than words can say!

*****

To my son, Ryan

Ryan, I am so sorry that you had to endure headaches from ages five and up. I am sorry that you did not feel well most of your preteen and teenage years. Yes, you have made mistakes, wasted time on worthless things, and hurt others with your selfish actions. I forgive you for any amount of pain that you have caused me and our family. I want you to know that the bad decisions you made *do not* define you. You are made by our Creator to do great things. The enemy knows this and wants to destroy you and your family in any way that he can. Forget what's behind and press forward with God. I have seen growth in you in the past ten months, and I have especially seen a strong determination in you in the last five months to tell your story and help thousands of people in the process. We are all "works in progress."

I know that you will persevere. I know that you will own your own business. I know that you will change the world with your ideas. God has given you a compassion for people and a deep desire to help them. I am proud of the fight that you have in you to overcome and proud of the man that you are becoming. As long as there is breath in my body, I will be here for you. I am so glad that God made you my son. I love you dearly, Ryan.

Red Flags to Look For

If you suspect a loved one is using drugs, here are some things to look for:

- change in behavior (Keep in mind, this is a normal teenage trait!);
- dropping grades;
- loss of interest in hobbies or activities;
- loss of appetite or weight loss;
- decrease in grooming habits;
- weird texts that don't make sense;
- irrational conversation;
- spending time with others who are up to no good;
- and having flesh-colored makeup in their room (guys).

Remember:

- Parent's intuition. When you sense there's *smoke*, check for a *fire*.
- Don't automatically dismiss anything that someone shares with you about what might be going on with your child. Investigate it.
- Above all, pray for God to give you wisdom and discernment.

When You Need Help

Turning Point Foundation (men's long- or short-term)
1881 County Road, 627 P.O. Box 448 Thorsby, Alabama 35171
turningpointal.org
(205) 646–3650 or (205) 281–3096 after hours

Revival Recovery Services (men's short-term)
Apple Valley, California
revivalrecoveryservices.com
(760) 887–1632
e-mail: info@revivalrecoveryservices.com

The Reprieve, Auburn, Alabama (long-term)
401 South 9th St., Opelika, Alabama 36801
thereprieve.com
(256) 783–1179
e-mail: reprieve@bradfordhealth.net

The Journey Detox and Recovery, LLC (detox facilities)
220 Hospital Drive, Jackson, Alabama 36545, (251) 246–1213
1330 Highway 231, Troy, Alabama 36081, (844) 585–5433
83825 Highway 9, Ashland, Alabama 36251, (256) 354–1121,
(800) 583–2197

Life's Most Important Question

Where will I spend eternity? The answer lies in Jesus Christ. Have you ever told a lie, stolen (no matter what the amount), or used God's name as a cuss word (blasphemy)? Have you lusted (adultery in your heart) after someone or hated someone without cause (murder in your heart)? If we're honest, we can all confess that we've broken God's law. Sin demands punishment just like in a court of law. Without proper payment for sin, we all stand guilty and think we deserve hell (eternal separation from God and anything that is good). Your sin debt must be paid for you to go free. The good news is that God sent Jesus into the world to live a perfect life, although He was tempted. He became the perfect sacrifice to die in our place. He was not only horrifically beaten, tortured, mocked, and killed to pay our sin debt, but He gloriously rose from the grave, defeating death and making a way for us to experience a fruitful life on earth and eventually a place with Him for all eternity. He paid your penalty in perfect blood to purchase your pardon because of His great love for you.

To be given eternal life with God, you must repent (confess and turn from your sins) and trust Jesus alone to save you. It is vital to know that after you repent and place your trust in Jesus as your Savior, you are not only a child of God, but also you are a *work in progress*. Difficult times will still come. You will experience grieving, discouragement, pain, and loss in life. But Jesus promises that He will never leave you and He will give you all that you need to fight every battle you engage in.

*****

To contact Josif about speaking:
e-mail: thewarwithinmystory@gmail.com

About the Author

Josif Wright is a retired public school educator and coach for twenty-eight years. He coached in over 1,300 baseball, softball, soccer, basketball, volleyball, and football games during his career.

He is currently touching lives as a hospice chaplain. By sharing his story, Josif's goal is to reach as many people as possible, showing them that there can be hope and redemption in this life, even in the most difficult of circumstances.

Josif enjoys sports and hunting. Josif and his wife Bethany have been married for twenty-eight years. They reside in Alabama with their two children, Ryan and Rebekah.

CPSIA information can be obtained
at www.ICGtesting.com
Printed in the USA
LVHW111346170519
618241LV00001B/67/P